CW00486489

LIFE IN THE LAST YEARS OF OLD AFRICA

THE GOOD AND BAD DEVILS OF SIERRA LEONE

1962 – 1965

&

LIFE IN HAILE SALESSIE'S ETHIOPIA

1969 – 1973

Douglas Holland

Copyright © 2023 Douglas Holland

Printed in the United States of America

All rights reserved. Except as permitted under the U.S. Copyright Act of 1976, no part of this publication may be reproduced, distributed, or transmitted in any form or by any means, or stored in a database or retrieval system, without the prior written permission of the publisher.

Editing & cover design: macarman6@gmail.com

Formatting: deboraklewis@yahoo.com

ISBN: 9798862615814

DEDICATION

Gerhart Clauda, an Austrian volunteer with such a strong compassion to help those with leprosy that he inspired all around him.

Rev Frank Hemsworth, a missionary for the English Methodist Church, raised funds, designed and supervised the building of Wesley Secondary School which still stands today.

Table of Contents

ACKNOWLEDGMENTS

As strangers in a foreign land, little could be done without supporting each other and without the support and kindness of the people we encountered. Any good that was done, any fearful situation that was overcome, was not accomplished alone. The risks were real, as were the difficulties, so my family and I wish to thank the many people who guided and helped us.

The Good

and

Bad Devils

of

Sierra Leone

1962 - 1965

PROLOGUE

The good and bad devils of Sierra Leone were there long before we arrived in 1961. No one knows their beginning or how long they had been a living part of African life. In the brief time we lived in Sierra Leone, we met them many times. Sadly, we saw their mystery destroyed and their roles come to an end.

The good devil was always dancing. He had his own drummer to beat the rhythms. His body was completely covered by a mask, colorful pads, and thatch. Even on a hot African day, he would dance, weaving and swaying to the drum beats.

The bad devils had no interest in dancing. Although clearly in the shape of men, their faces were covered with cloth and their bodies with thatch. They had no hands, but protruding from the thatch on each arm was a stick, sticks that forced obedience. They too had a helper, but his hands held not a drum, but a large pan for receiving "donations". Because of the fear of these devils, their power appeared unlimited.

The worst devils were not those in the physical world but those on the inside. The bad devils may look intimidating, but they could be pacified with the appropriate gifts. The devils on the inside could entice with promise of wealth and power and take over your life. They are more to be feared.

These stories took place long before the tragic history of Sierra Leone had unfolded. The brutality of Sierra Leone's wars and the ravage of Ebola made the place where we lived feel like an enchanted, but lost world.

CHAPTER 1
ARRIVAL IN FREETOWN

This is a story of a very young family: my wife Betty Lu, our four-month-old daughter Jackie and your story teller, Doug. Sierra Leone was called the white man's grave, but we came to Africa convinced that God would protect us. Africa was young in spirit at that time, full of great potential. Colonial rule was ending, and Africa was free to find its own way. We proudly believed that, if they followed our American way, they would join us as prosperous countries.

To us, Africa was an exotic place as described by African students or by returning missionaries. However, on that day in 1962 when we looked down from our plane window, we realized this was not a story-book place but for real. We were going to live in this very foreign land for the next three years. My wife and I chose to come; our little four-month-old daughter did not. But for the next three years, the three of us would be living in a little village like the ones we could see below.

We landed in Senegal on a steel-mesh runway. There was no grand airport to meet us, only a few buildings and the African bush. Civil servants politely inspected our documents. They did not need assault rifles, but that time would come. Next stop, Freetown.

Freetown was founded for liberated slaves that were returned to Africa. Their language, Creole, blended the colonial languages they brought with them with the local languages. At first it made little sense, but it seemed to grow on you and eventually we depended on it to get around. Our first view of the city was across the water that separated the airport from the city. From a distance, the city was beautiful. Up close, it disclosed the gritty sights, sounds and odors of a vibrant African city. In this city was the English Methodist Rest House where we were brought.

Our first cultural clash occurred in this rest house, not with the African culture but with the English. The English people we met there were good people who endured life in Africa to make it a better place. Why else would they live for years in a malarial-infested place with such an inhospitable climate? However, to young Americans like us, they seemed a bit condescending to Africans. Our feelings came to a head at the first dinner when they rang a little bell to summon servants to serve the dinner. We were appalled but too courteous to say anything. After a few more excellent dinners served by servants summoned by the tingle of the bell, we were not so critical. When we were alone together, we vowed never to have servants and certainly, never to have a bell. However, for the next three years, we also hired workers for household, but we always summoned them by calling their names. Finally, we departed upcountry to the village of Segbwema.

CHAPTER 2
INTO THE INTERIOR

Our driver and guide to the roadways of Sierra Leone was Miss. Driscoll, the principal of the Njaluahun Girls' School where we were going to teach for the next three years. Although the school was English Methodist, she held this prestigious position while being an American and an American Wesleyan Methodist. Following British tradition, it could be a school run by missionaries with salaries paid by the Sierra Leonean government. She held the position because, unlike me, she was an experienced administrator who knew exactly how to get things done. She was a confident lady and generous with Fanta, an orange drink I would later come to hate after a disastrous mountain climb.

The way from Freetown to Segwema starts on narrow paved roads but a long stretch at the end is a track of red clay called laterite. This was the end of the rainy season, and the road was a series of mud holes. The unbreakable rule for successfully getting through is to never slow down. After three years, I was admired by all for my ability to do this with the school car. We owned a car for a while but decided that only a well-funded institution could afford the cost of maintenance. After navigating the muddy road, we finally got to see the school.

What a relief it was to see this beautiful school! It was clean and neat with beautiful landscaping and whitewashed buildings. It had a gas-motor-driven pump to bring water to our staff house. So what if the source was a swamp and the motor did not always work? We even had hot water piped in from a barrel with burning wood under it. Our refrigerator worked on kerosene. We never developed the skill needed to make that work well. Our cook stove used propane. Everything was fine except for lights. We had to depend on kerosene lanterns. This was not good for teachers, grading papers in a hot climate by sitting very close to such a source of heat as those lanterns. At that point we had not been introduced to giant cockroaches and rats in the house and the army ants and deadly green mambas on the outside.

School would not start for a month, and this seemed like a long time for us living in the bush with nothing to do. A young man named Bobo, from the small village nearby, adopted us and was our guide to how to survive in Africa for the hopelessly unprepared. We were struggling to learn Mende, and he was our teacher and translator, mostly translator. He arranged a steady supply of fruit and vegetables. From this Bobo may have profited or he may have been kind and helpful, we will never know. Anyway, he showed us around the village and farms and was our window to rural village life.

In fact, Bobo may have saved us from serious harm by the army ants. The hunting technique used by the local army ants was to travel in lines about an inch wide to a new area. Once there, they spread out into a wide front and proceeded to eat everything in their path that could not escape. Although they are about a half-inch in size, they will build up in numbers on a small animal until it is completely covered with ants. When the animal cannot move, they will eat it on the spot down to the skeleton. I watched a frog die this way. Since these ants do not swim, Bobo taught us to put the four legs of Jackie's crib in tin cans filled with water to protect her during the night. One day, army ants were headed in their narrow line directly to our house. Bobo arranged with some villagers to burn a line between the ants and us, to turn them away. Army ants did affect our lives, especially the life of our cat. But that story comes later.

We were quickly exposed to the cruelty of life on the edge of poverty. Bobo got us involved with a small village near us and we soon became the village clinic for cuts and fevers. One day, a man appeared from the village and asked us to come: someone was seriously sick. We visited the sick person. He was rolling on the floor in severe pain, coughing up dark blood. We were helpless but said we would go into the hospital the next day and get some medicine. During the night we heard the start of wailing from the village and knew the man had died. We were invited to the funeral. A good devil danced for the grieving family and friends. He was good because his only purpose in being there was to relieve the pain of grieving through his dancing. In fact, the funeral turned into a celebration with food and dancing. Later I asked the missionary doctor at the hospital about the man. He said the man had come in with a serious case of TB. Treatment was expensive and the man and his family could not afford it. He had to die in front of his family because of the lack of a few dollars. For a while, we were angry with the missionary doctors for not helping this family. In time, we too were rationing our help like the hospital, giving it only to those who were young and most likely to benefit.

CHAPTER 3
THE NJALUAHUN GIRLS

Living in the bush was not very exciting, so we were very happy when the school girls appeared and classes began. We now had a chance to put into practice our more enlightened treatment of Africans. First, rather than hire a servant, we employed two students, Isattu and Beindu, who needed the money for school fees and a young man, Alamu, to take care of Jackie. Isattu and Beindu had one bedroom and we and Jackie had the other. That actually worked out well. Second, we decided to break tradition and eat lunch with the girls in the school once a week. They ate rice topped with a sauce made of potato leaves, tomato, onion, hot peppers and dried fish. We had no idea how hot West African peppers could be and how much the girls loved these peppers—they even brought more to add to the sauce! We tried bringing larger and larger bottles of water, but we could only last one semester before we discreetly stopped showing up.

The schoolgirls were perfect students, respectful and eager to learn. The girls were a mix of Christian and Muslim and a mix of tribal groups as well, but they seemed to get along with each other just fine. We kept them busy with classes, homework, clubs, sports and plays.

The only immediate problem was that they could not understand American English. Even the simple instructions, like 'please sit', did not seem to register. After a few months, the problem seemed to go away. I think we subconsciously started mimicking the English accent and it took us about three months to do it. When we returned to the US, we were accused of arrogantly speaking in a British accent, which we did not know we were doing.

As a country boy with a science background, I knew nothing about the classics of English literature. They put me in charge of the literature club. Although the girls were normally shy, they loved plays and were natural actresses. Therefore, the literature club regaled the school with plays and literary readings. Living in a boarding school is demanding since the students always needed attention to keep them out of trouble. We loved it, since living in such an isolated place so far from home would have otherwise been unbearable.

The girls needed all those acting skills to get along in their rapidly changing world. In their home village, they were living in ancient Africa. Life changes very slowly. In the school, they were in another world, a world of modern technology and new cultural norms. I am sure they had a hard time understanding who they really were. In remote villages there were no radios, electric lights, books and little food variety. Everything centered around raising crops and children. One word would describe the reaction of a modern young person, "boring". But boring is the wrong word. Life for these young girls was marred by superstitious fears and cultural customs that control young women. When most girls approached sexual maturity, they joined the secret Bundu Society. They learned how to behave as wives and mothers and performed dances in public. The dark side is that they were subjected to female circumcision. We think that most of the schoolgirls did not do this, but we are not sure. Some of the ones that did frequently missed school because of infection

One afternoon, there was a commotion in the dorms and a girl disappeared. Other girls said she was called down to the swamp by a devil. We went down there only to find her completely hysterical. It took several of us to get her back to the school. It was a scene out of the Bible, devil possession, but where was there someone who could cast out the demon? In the absence of Jesus or his disciples, I was afraid someone would ask me to do it. Instead, the Headmistress wisely sent for a doctor from the hospital, and he came and gave her an injection of a tranquilizer. Afterwards, she calmly and vividly described the devil that possessed her. Unfortunately, the devil would not stay away. Finally, the girl had to be sent home. We and the hospital had no way to treat mental illness.

The other girls understood her. They had seen devils as well, but the devils were not so strong. The girls told us that the devils were always white.

CHAPTER 4
FIRST CHRISTMAS IN AFRICA

Good devils are likely to appear at any public occasion and Christmas is not an exception. Christmas is a time when African leaders like to give gifts to their loyal supporters who keep them in their lucrative offices, black Mercedes, and nice homes. A good devil weaving and swaying to the intoxicating drumbeat is a gift that all can enjoy.

As Americans in an African state that was emerging from British rule, we were a little out of place. Even though Sierra Leone had just declared independence, there were still plenty of British people around. The small village of Segbwema had a British banker, several missionaries and a hospital with several doctors and nurses. For Jackie's first birthday party, there were about 11 children near her age, all of them white. We mixed comfortably with the British, but we were there to meet the Africans. Thus, when the Christmas social time arrived, we accepted invitations to both British and African gatherings. The British were kind and included us but failed to brief us on the intricacies of Christmas customs. As a result, we did not show up with presents at the time required. Worst for me personally, I found a coin in my Christmas pudding. Glad that I did not swallow it, I hid it away so as not to embarrass our host. After dinner, the host was puzzled why the coin that was deliberately put in the pudding was not reported. I was horrified that I had to admit my complete ignorance of this strange custom and turned in the coin to receive a special gift.

The African party was something altogether different than we expected. The party was hosted by Maigore Kallon, a member of Parliament for our area. He chose a cool, dark wood on the bank of a river near Daru. There were delegations from the many chiefdoms in our area. Each of the chiefs was given a cow, a large bag of rice and a large tin of palm oil, the necessary ingredients for a lavish feast. The chiefs could either prepare the feast on the spot or return home later and then prepare a feast. There were several different groups of women, and each group was beautifully dressed in the identical material. The pattern and color of the material indicated they were all from the same town. They had made the dresses to honor their host, Mr. Kallon.

Our friend Bobo was our guide. He led us through masses singing and dancing people to an archway made of branches and guarded by a policeman. The policeman let us in, and we met a friend of ours, Mr. Bow the head of the primary school in Segwema. He introduced us to Mr. Kallon and to the paramount chiefs who were there. When speaking with Mr. Kallon, we found he was educated in the US. He was very articulate and seemed to have a sound idea of how Sierra Leone could move ahead in development. I was amazed at how quickly this man seemed to have mastered both the ways of the modern world and still have the skill to win support he needed from the traditional culture.

The good devils were all around. It seemed that in these cool and dark woods on the river, the fear of devils was replaced by a joy in their presence.

CHAPTER 5
VILLAGE AND SCHOOL LIFE IN AFRICA

Life was tenuous in the villages. Children could become ill with a fever and die. Food supplies could be stolen. Serious injuries could occur. Rains could come late, or storms could wash away the crops. People did what they could to ward off these evils. Children wore amulets for protection and their hair was cut except for a topknot so God could yank them upwards to heaven. Spiritual teachers were consulted. And people prayed for protection from the evil that was all around. Life for staff and students held many of the same concerns. Illness was primary but there were other concerns about isolation, money, and failure. Religion, either Islam or Christian, was a source of hope and comfort.

Agriculture was regulated by the two major seasons, the rainy season, and the dry season. During the rainy season, it rained pretty much every day until you were praying for it to stop. Then in the dry season, it did not rain at all until, sick of the heat and dust, you reversed yourself and prayed for rain. Unfortunately, these heavy tropical rains were deadly to the topsoil. The only way to farm was to allow bush to grow on the land for about six years to build up at least a thin layer of topsoil. Then the bush is burned, and the soil is used for a few years before it is all washed away.

The burning of the bush started near our house a few weeks before the dry season was to end. The men in the village would work together to burn each family's plot. They were experts at controlling the fires. After the burned wood cooled, work would continue with removal of some of the roots. At this point, the farm work would be handed over to the women. When the rains started, the women had the hard and tedious work of planting the crops, mostly hill-grown rice, and raising chickens. However, everyone in the family worked. The children carried firewood and water, the men built the farm structures and homes and the grandparents contributed by making things for the family. Almost nothing was purchased since this was subsistence living with little chance of earning money.

Measured by numbers, our life at the Girls' school seemed to expand. Beindu and Isattu helped with the housework. Betty Lu and I were both teaching full time and staff houses did not have the conveniences we depended on at home. We also hired a young man to do some of the heavy work like securing water, firewood and heating the water for baths. All three were attracted to Jackie, so she was hopelessly spoiled. In addition to the seven people, we adopted a baby squirrel, two rabbits and a monkey. The monkey was not interested in us except as a source of food, but it did seem to like Jackie, perhaps because they were both at the same level on the floor.

Betty Lu's parents were not happy about our taking Jackie to Africa. She was their first and only grandchild so far. *Our* greatest fear was malaria. Along with us, she took a weekly tablet that was supposed to suppress malaria. It had a bitter taste, so we hid it in mashed banana. To this day, Jackie will not eat bananas. We all slept under mosquito nets. Jackie had her own in her crib. Minor bouts of stomach problems and fever were common. The organization that arranged our stay gave us a large number of little green pills for such problems. They seemed to work, but we used them all within a year. Fortunately, by that time we seemed to have adjusted to local germs and didn't need them. Jackie did have two serious bouts with Tumbu flies. These flies lay eggs on clothes hanging on the line. When the clothes are worn, the eggs hatch and larvae burrow into the skin and start to grow. When the larvae are about a half-inch in size, they work their way out of your skin and go off into the world to cause more problems.

To prevent this, all underwear, diapers, clothes, and bedding needed to be ironed. Not having electricity, we used a charcoal iron that was very heavy. Twice somehow, a diaper didn't get ironed, and the larvae were not killed. Poor Jackie had about a dozen larvae growing under her skin. I was told that if squeezed towards their entry hole, the larvae would pop out. In the evening I laid Jackie on a bed and tried it. Much to my surprise it worked. Knowing that if one broke inside there would be serious trouble, I cautiously continued until all were successfully removed. Before it was finished, Jackie was sleeping soundly.

CHAPTER 6
CHRISTIAN, MUSLIMS AND TRADITIONAL RELIGION

All in our little world around Segbwema were deeply religious. We had to be since life was so uncertain. All understood the difficulty of preparing for a future over which we had little control. A personal religious faith, Christian, Muslim, or traditional, provided a sense of comfort that allowed enjoyment of everyday life.

Our students were a mix of the three religions. My wife and I led a club for some of the Christian girls called Scripture Union. In a very honest discussion, the girls insisted they could not see a difference between the Christian and Muslim religions. I think they saw that each inside trusted their God to love and care for them. The tremendously different history and theological beliefs did not seem very important to them. I wish I could say that I was as enlightened as they were at that time in my life.

The Methodist Primary School has the only level open field in town, their football field. At the end of Ramadan, the Muslims needed a large open space for their prayers. When prayer time came, the Muslims occupied the Methodist field. I never found out if anyone gave them permission or if they even needed permission. It seemed so natural that the field was ideal and needed so, why not! Even to this day, the religious communities in these African villages get along together.

CHAPTER 7
LIFE IN SEGBWEMA

After the first year, a school for boys was started near the town of Segbwema, so our family moved into town and lived on the Methodist mission compound. At first, classes were held in the Methodist church sanctuary. American Peace Corps teachers came and lived in the town. The schoolboys, like the girls, were a mix of religions. Every day started with a chapel service led by the staff. Our staff included a Methodist, Southern Baptist, Catholic, Jew and two Presbyterians. As headmaster, I asked each to give short sermons in the chapel. We all took our turn and I doubt that the students had any idea of our different faiths.

Our new home was quite attractive with whitewashed houses and beautiful trees and shrubs set in large grass lawns. Large overhanging roofs kept the sun out and the windows, totally devoid of glass or screen, allowed the cool breezes inside. The house was spacious but made of chicka (wood and mud) which long before had been invaded with termites. These industrious little insects would produce large hemispherical mud protrusions from the walls. After the rains started, the termites would produce a generation of future queens with wings that would fly off looking for a new home. Since we had no screens, the house would be littered with them. We used a high-tech kerosene lamp with a mantle and a glass chimney for light. Like the locals, we found that these termites could be roasted in the hot air rising from the chimney to make popcorn like treat.

Although the houses were well designed for the tropics, two features made them unsafe. The lack of screens exposed us to mosquitos during the evening and morning. Malaria was rampant; Sierra Leone was not called the white man's grave for nothing. The beds were covered with mosquito nets, but you had to come out sometimes. Poor Jackie had to take bitter malaria pills hidden in banana. The malaria pills seemed to suppress the disease, but we carried the microbes with us to the US and came down with malaria there.

The second dangerous feature involved the beautiful trees, shrubs, and grass. We had a family of green mambas in our front yard. Green mambas are deadly and aggressive. We purchased a pet mongoose to protect us. Mongooses are easily domesticated and this one was soon into everything. One time during a staff meeting in my house, a dignified Sierra Leonean teacher had the misfortune to have the mongoose sneak up behind him and run up his pant leg. It was not a very dignified moment for him. The church was near our house and a few weeks later the mongoose came into the church in the middle of the sermon. As he circled the pastor a few times, while the congregation watched expectantly. To my relief, the mongoose returned to the door he came in, and left.

The green mambas and the mongoose seemed to ignore each other. Finally, we took matters into our own hands. We gathered several men with long sticks and surrounded the bush with the green mamba. Then we tossed the mongoose into the bush. He apparently smelled the snake and started his tic-tic-tic sound. When the mamba heard the sound, he shot out of the bush and passed through our circle before any of us could move. The mongoose seemed relieved that the snake was gone.

We heard our mongoose was caught stealing food from a neighbor and ended up being invited for dinner as the main course. We all remained a safe distance from that shrub in the future.

Segbwema was a commercial center of sorts. There was an open-air market for food and once a week, a cow would be driven down from the north by a Fulani trader and butchered. There were Lebanese shops for packaged foods, building supplies and rice. The town even had a bank with a European manager. The Methodist's operated a large hospital with several European doctors and nurses. The paramount chief with his traditional court was in the center of town.

The European-American community was diverse, composed of missionaries, doctors and nurses, teachers, bankers, and traders. The entire group hardly ever came together except for children's birthday parties.

I did have an opportunity to experience justice in the traditional courts. We had a male worker caring for the school facilities. When I collected the school fees, these were locked in a box that was locked in a room. We could not afford a proper safe. The money was stolen and the only person that had access to the place was our worker. He was arrested and the trial was held in the local court. The building was open on all sides with only a roof to keep off the rain. I was provided with an interpreter since I could not speak Mende, the local language. Mende is a tonal language and the slightest difference in tone totally changes the meaning of a word. I only knew of one foreigner that could speak it and he was an unmarried man living alone in a small village. The court ruled in favor of the worker, and it was explained to me that we lacked any positive proof that he was guilty. I am not sure I agreed with the verdict, but you cannot deny that all was done with great transparency, and everyone had a chance to speak.

The Lebanese and the British army were both were very helpful to us. Only in the Lebanese shop could we get such essentials as cornflakes and toothpaste. They also had the building materials we needed to build our new school and they gave the school discounts as well. My barber was Lebanese, and he used a nasty looking straight razor to shave my neck. I learned very quickly not to discuss Israel with him.

The British army lived in Daru, an even smaller village than Segbwema but nearby. They had an officer's club with a swimming pool. The officer's club had a movie night every week. Since we were totally without any other entertainment, not even a radio, we eagerly accepted their generous invitation to attend. This was only a year or two since independence so you might wonder why the British army was still in Sierra Leone. The rumor was that the Sierra Leonean army was well armed with rifles, but the British had the bullets. Apparently, this changed in a few years when Sierra Leone set a new record for changes of government in one year. For Americans, the British officer's club was a strange place in the middle of the bush. The officers were strictly dressed to their code and were very proper in their behavior. One time an officer pulled me aside to give me some firm advice. "In the British Army we wear ties" he told me. All the male teachers had to secure ties from somewhere and wear them in the hot tropical movie night.

CHAPTER 8
THE UNFORTUNATE END
OF THE BAD DEVILS

With sadness, we witnessed the end of a tradition that could have gone back hundreds of years. The bad devils appeared on occasions to enforce orderly behavior in the local population. Their power was based primarily on fear of the supernatural and to a lesser extent on the heavy sticks they had in place of hands. They did abuse their power by extracting food or small donations of money, but this was not of very great consequence under normal circumstances. An event happened to make the circumstances far from normal.

The paramount chief died. This is a major event in a traditional society since it brings insecurity and fear. The bad devils came out to keep order. Each devil had a man with him with a large metal dish. At first all was quiet, and life continued as normal. The devils started blocking the only road through town and extracting money to let people pass. They would pound on the hood of the car with sticks and their man with the bowl would demand coins. We were not immune from this but, to us, the amounts were not significant. Things got more serious when they started stealing chickens from the local people. The local police told them to stop, and they retaliated by beating the policemen and kidnapping the police chief, talking him into the bush.

Eventually our army friends from Daru showed up with armed soldiers. Later riot police from Kenema came with a large truck. They captured each of the bad devils, removed his mask and put him in the truck. The truck took them to a base in Kenema, about 40 miles away. The chief of police was returned. We never saw the devils again. I think removing the masks was all that was needed to end the tradition. When people saw they were only men, probably local men they knew, the bad devil's power was gone.

CHAPTER 9
THE FIRST DAYS OF THE NEW BOY'S SCHOOL

Frank Himsworth, the head of the Methodist Mission, designed the new school. I designed the new staff house. Since neither of us had any training in construction, I think he over designed the supporting pillars. The walls were made with blocks made from a recipe using termite mounds with a little cement. The recipe and block making machine were donated by CARE and much of the labor was donated by students and staff. As a result of the massive pillars, this building is still standing even after the terrible civil war that destroyed almost everything, including my staff house.

The school and staff house were built in a coffee plantation about a mile out of town. The staff house was designed as a duplex but only one half was completed. The other half became a badly needed classroom. For our students, walking that mile was easy but not for us. We had briefly owned a blue VW 62 beetle, but the repair costs proved more than I could afford. Returning from Freetown with the whole family, the engine self-destructed. After a long tow back to Freetown, we were told there were no rebuilt engines in Freetown, but they were coming from Germany. We had to return to Segwema and come back later by train, trips of over 10 hours each. That was the last straw, and the car was sold to a new teacher.

This was not a good time to be without a car. Betty Lu was pregnant, and the hospital was two miles away. We had no communications and no transportation. We had no plan A or plan B. Apparently, God cares for the careless. Christmas was coming and we were invited to a Christmas performance in a school on the other side of town. The invitation came with transportation. As we were driving past the hospital, Betty Lu said she felt a little strange. We asked to be dropped off. I took Jackie home and returned to the hospital to welcome our new son Daniel Saffa. Saffa means first son in Mende. He received a proper English pram which, after a little repair, was quite luxurious. Since both Betty Lu and I had heavy teaching loads, we hired an older man, Sar, to take care of our household. Dan really liked Sar and Sar brought his young daughter to play with Jackie.

Building out in the raw bush has some dangers. Crime was a minor concern then, but army ants were a much more important concern. We found a new way to protect ourselves. The ants would not cross kerosene so when we saw them coming, we put a streak of kerosene on the doorsteps. In case we were sleeping, the legs of the cribs where our children slept were placed in a large tin can filled with water and the cribs were kept away from any furniture that could form a bridge. Unlike our old mission house, I had designed our windows with screens that kept the ants out. I remember the first attack. We saw many small creatures rushing past our house. Then we saw what happened to the slower ones, they were coated with large army ants with their pinchers holding on to them.

We had a white cat that was almost wild. It would on rare occasions show up for some food. In one attack, we heard a loud screech, and the cat came racing into the house covered with army ants. Apparently, it had been sleeping on the ground. The ants were holding on to his skin, around his eyes and in his ears. I filled a bucket with water and, holding the cat by its nose, I pushed him into the water. Everything was covered but his nose. The cat had no fight in him. After several minutes the ants floated to the surface and I removed the cat, free of ants. I know this is hard to believe, but that cat's personality was completely changed. He was transformed from a wild roaming cat to an affectionate house cat.

Our new location had a few houses around and it had its own local chief. He was very helpful. Most of the day he would lie in a hammock on the porch in front of his house. I had planted a small vegetable garden in front of my house and was often working in the garden. One day he got up from his hammock and came to give me some good advice. He said that the men in the village would not respect me if they saw me working in the garden. Real men would get their wives to do it or hire someone. I hired someone.

The chief's wife was hired as our cook for "CARE Cakes." These were delicious cakes made from the free ingredients we got from CARE. The Peace Corps had developed a wonderful recipe using local peppers, onions, and spices. She would deep fry the cakes and distribute them to the boys. These cakes were so good that we used to have minor food riots at mealtimes. The boys mimicked an ad of the times and would say "Real men prefer CARE Cakes." The wife of the chief had no trouble controlling our students, so all went smoothly. Although these cakes were only intended for needy people, the cakes were so good that the staff were allowed to eat a few.

CHAPTER 10
TRAVEL IN SIERRA LEONE

Not only were the roads in our area not paved, but they also consisted of a red clay, slippery when wet. In the rainy season, the road was a series of muddy puddles of unknown depth. Public transportation was mainly by begging rides on trucks large enough to manage the roads. As a result, we made very few trips but the ones we made were always interesting.

One trip was to the diamond mining area, not to see the large foreign mining operation but to visit the small local mines. The diamonds are found in gravel that is below a few feet of mud in swamps. A circular spot would be cleared before the digging would start. A bucket was suspended on a rope between two men, one on each side of the cleared area. By rhythmically working the ropes, they scoop water from their hole and throw it some distance away. In this way, they could control the level of water in their hole. This would allow men with metal pans to scoop up gravel and, by swirling the water in the pan, find any diamonds. They showed us a small one they had found. This operation was probably not legal since the diamonds found their way directly to diamond dealers without any government taxes. It was muddy work but not dangerous and everybody seemed to be having a good time. This was long before the civil war and the term "blood diamonds" was applied to these diamonds.

The Moa River was only about 5 miles away, too far to walk, but on occasions we could catch rides. I had a fishing rod, so I tried some lures in the river. Much to my surprise, and also the surprise of the locals, I caught some very large bass-like fish. Some were so big they would swim away with my lure and never surface.

I wanted to explore the Moa but the jungle around it was impenetrable. One of the young teachers from England, John Dransfield, was very interested in insect life in the tropics so he and I hatched up a plan. Several miles up-stream was another place where a road reached the river. We decided to purchase a dugout canoe from someone there and float it down the river. All started well. We got the boat for a good price and equipped it with a camera and plastic bags for specimens. Betty Lu was waiting for us down stream. We shoved off and all was well for about half the trip. Then we saw a half-submerged tree ahead. Dugout canoes do not maneuver very well, and we hit it head on. The boat was carried under the tree with me still in it. John wisely jumped onto the tree. Fortunately, I did not get caught on the many branches under the water and I emerged on the upriver side of the tree. I joined my friend sitting on this tree surrounded by impenetrable rainforest with our canoe under the water and pinned to the tree. We still had one paddle and with that we pried the canoe loose and managed to pour out most of the water. We proceeded to the place where Betty Lu was waiting. She said that the plastic bags had preceded us, so she was more than a little worried. We left our canoe on the shore and thankfully, never saw it again.

We did swim in the river even though the locals warned us not to. We found out why. While resting on the sandy shore, we noticed what appeared to be a log moving in the water. Once we realized that it was floating up the river, we recognized it as a large crocodile. We then understood why the locals would not let their children go in the water. We never went into the water again.

Travel in Sierra Leone was mostly thorough high bush with limited views. We longed for the open Arizona deserts so in the summer we headed for the beaches of Freetown. The palm trees, sand and surf were glorious. Jackie would have nothing to do with the surfing part but eventually allowed us to carry her into the ocean. While in Freetown, we decided to get on the Mail Boat that traveled the West African coast. Although the name sounds humble, it was actually and respectable English cruise ship. The dinners were formal, necktie and assigned seats and, of course, without children. Children were fed first and then detained in a playroom. Jackie, not being an English child, would have nothing to do with that. She made everyone in the playroom suffer a full hour of screaming.

We went as far as Ghana where we enjoyed travel by minibus. Clearly Nkrumah's was the hero of the Ghanaian people. His pictures were everywhere. School kids would march and sing his praises. We were very surprised when later he was replaced with hardly a fuss.

The two most memorable trips were both attempts to climb the mountains of Sierra Leone. The difficulty in climbing these mountains was not their height or steepness but just getting to them through the swamps and rainforest. The first trip was to the second highest mountain with two young teachers from England, John Dransfield, survivor of the canoe trip, and Clive Hobson. We backpacked in but the trip in was very difficult, and we arrived at the base of the mountain without time left for a proper assault. Even though it was too late to climb, Clive insisted on making a try. John and I set up camp and waited for his return. This was a totally wild area with only rainforest as far as we could see. After night fell, he still had not returned. John felt too sick to travel, so I set out with a flashlight to find the missing teacher. The Vegetation was so high that the path was like a tunnel, a very dark tunnel. When my light started to dim, I turned back. All ended well when Clive showed up the next morning. He had found a large rock and climbed onto the rock and spent the night there. John felt well enough to hike out. We survived a walk in the dark jungle, a night on a rock and an illness in a remote place but only Clive climbed the mountain.

The next year, I decided to try again but this time attempt the highest mountain in Sierra Leone, Bintumani. This mountain was only 6, 400 feet high but is in an isolated rainforest. The group was larger since it included two new teachers from England and three Peace Corps teachers. John and Clive had returned to

England. We also had the Peace Corps Land Rover. We were more organized and arranged for some local men to carry much of our stuff. We also picked up a guide along the way whose name was John Bull. Again, the way was long and difficult, passing swamps and streams. Since this place had never been explored for minerals, I took along a Geiger counter. We were delayed when our carriers refused to continue into another tribal area. We had to find new carriers. Again, we were late getting to the mountain base. We set up a camp and started up, hoping we could make it up and back in what was left of the day. About mid-afternoon, we emerged from the rainforest into an open grass plain where we could see the jungle far below and the mountain top above us. The top looked tantalizingly close to me. Standing in the grass, an argument broke out. Two of us wanted to continue to the top and spend the night there. John Bull thought some French climbers may have constructed a thatch hut there a few weeks earlier. With no food and no certainty of shelter, the others wanted to go back. Finally, we split up. Martin Puryur and I with John Bull decided to go to the top and spend the night there. We thought perhaps those French climbers may have left some food. The others would return to the base camp and wait until noon before heading out. School was starting in two days and almost all the teaching staff was there on the mountain.

The top was farther than we thought so Martin, John and I arrived at the base of a rock cap at sunset. John was right about the thatch hut but there was no food. It was a long cold night, and in the morning, I had some serious stomach cramps. Martin insisted I climb the cap stone with him, and he literally pushed me to the top. We recorded our names in a glass bottle secured there and started down. I was in a lot of pain, but we went slowly down arriving in the village at the base just as it was getting dark. The others had left on the long hike to the Land Rover. They left no food.

This was a very poor village. They had no food but pumpkin soup which they generously shared with us. They gave us a hut to sleep in for the night. In the morning, it was clear that the men in the village were agitated. Apparently, they were concerned that I would die, and they would be blamed for it. They put together a stretcher made from poles and with me in it, we set off. In the afternoon we came upon some fruit and after eating some, I felt good enough to walk. By evening we arrived at the village where we had left the Land Rover. They had left without us. There was a Lebanese shop in the village, so we went there. When he saw us, he had pity on us and took us into his house, gave us warm Fanta, fed us and let us stay the night. In the morning, he found a truck going to Segbwema which we gladly took. At this point Martin became ill and was in pain all the way home.

My wife was relieved to see me. She had reported to school the day before and the others were there, but no one would say what had happened to Martin and me. Perhaps they did the right thing to leave us. They had classes to teach, and Martin and I were old enough to take care of ourselves. Anyway, there were no hard feelings, and we were always good friends.

CHAPTER 11
THE WESLEY BOYS

At the age of 24, I was in charge of a boys school with about 200 students. They were respectful but as young boys, could not always avoid trouble. However, I never encountered a mean boy. One of my responsibilities was to discipline misbehavior. We were trying to clear our new soccer field of stumps, so my standard punishment was to remove a stump. The boys did not mind because they loved soccer and really wanted a soccer field.

The most serious problem occurred off campus in the town at night. One of our older boys (probably only a few years younger than me) got into a fight with a primary school teacher. Based on his story and some witnesses, I decided there was an equal fault and did nothing. This set off a storm of protest from all the primary teachers and they demanded that I appear before them. I was told in a scathing tone that failure to expel a student that fought with a teacher would destroy our disciplinary system and education would turn to chaos. Finally, after they were exhausted, I left. The student did remove a few stumps, but he was not expelled. Failure to get an education meant life as a peasant farmer and I could not do that to any student. My stature in the eyes of the students rose quite a bit, which was appreciated considering how young I was.

Like the girls, the boys loved to perform in plays. They all seemed born to be actors. Even though they seldom had the chance to speak English out of school, they knew how to act out anything from serious drama to comedy. In general, we kept the girls and boys apart, but one exception was theater. Plays with boys and girls were performed at both the boys and girl school. All the staff enjoyed them.

Sports was another passion for our boys. Soccer as well as track and field were both given serious attention. The only other school to play against was the Catholic school. Since the Head Priest and the head of the Methodist Mission were occasional dinner partners, they arranged matches. The matches were fiercely contested. The field and track occurred on a special day devoted to sports. Each event was carefully refereed and eagerly watched.

The teaching staff were highly motivated, and the quality of education was high. The students worked hard and did well on their outside examinations. They were educationally well prepared. Since Sierra Leone was newly independent, they were patriotic and excited about the future.

CHAPTER 12
THE PRESENT

After we returned to America, Sierra Leone enjoyed several peaceful years. This was followed by years of unrest and then the brutal civil war. The ugliness of the fighting was graphically reported in the movie "Blood Diamonds".

We were never able to keep track of our students, but we did get reports from the English Methodist Mission. The beautiful girl's school and my staff house were destroyed. Under dense vines, the staff house floor can be found with tiny footprints of a little white child, Jackie. The boy's school was badly damaged, but it was restored and still operates. Those over designed pillars were needed in the end.

The hospital where our son was born was almost destroyed in the war. It was restored, at least as a clinic. Little remains the place our son entered the world. Segbwema was in the middle of the Ebola outbreak. We heard the clinic was closed due to Ebola. How sad that such good people should suffer so much.

I suppose no one understands the cause of the war and cruelty of the people who we enjoyed living with for three years. Perhaps it is evidence of the bad devils inside waiting. The lure of the diamonds brought them to the surface for people with little income and living perilous lives.

Chapter 1: Arrival in Africa

Chapter 1: Arrival in Freetown

Chapter 2: Jackie's friend

Chapter 3: Bundu girls

Chapter 3: Into the interior

Chapter 3: Jackie with students

Njaluahun School

Chapter 3: The students

Chapter 5: Little wildlife escaped this fate

Chapter 5: Making cloth

Chapter 6: Praying on Methoist Fields

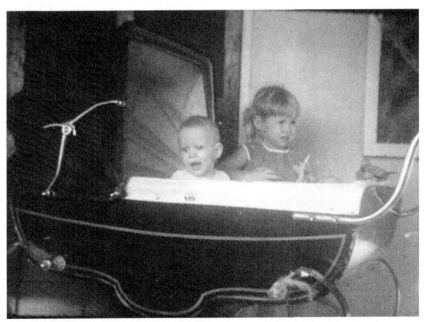

Chapter 7: Dan's fancy pram

Chapter 7: Jackie and friends

Chapter 7: Life in Segbwema

Chapter 7: Punishment was to clear a football field

Chapter 7: Segbwema's main street

Chapter 7: Shopping in Segbwema

Chapter 7: The cat that was almost eaten by army ants

Chapter 9: Boy's school

Chapter 9: Lebanese owner of store that helped build the school

Chapter 9: Main building

Chapter 9: Prime Minister visits boy's school

Chapter 9: Staff housing

Chapter 9: Superintendent and school builder

Chapter 9: Water supply for staff house

Chapter 10: Basecamp for climbing highest peak

Chapter 10: Informal diamond mining

Chapter 10: Informal diamond mining

Chapter 10: Low camp for mountain climbing

Chapter 10: Most turn back from climb

Chapter 10: Sierra Leone ocean beaches

Chapter 11: Joint play

Chapter 11: Sports racing

Chapter 11: Unfinished staff house with classroom for Betty

LIFE

IN

HAILE SALESSIE'S

ETHIOPIA

1969 - 1973

PROLOGUE

Ethiopians date their history back to Solomon, King of Israel. The visit of the Queen of Sheba to Solomon resulted in a son Menelik, the first emperor of Ethiopia. Haile Selassie, the last emperor of Ethiopia, was considered to be a direct descendant. Actually, Ethiopia is a diverse country with many tribes and languages. Their food, language, music, dances and art are unique. The Ethiopians we knew were mostly Amhara and Tigrinya, the dominate ethnic groups at that time. Ethiopians are a proud people, not only because of their heritage but also for withstanding European attempts to colonize them. As Americans, we are also proud of our heritage and history. I think that these shared attitudes make it easy to establish good friendships and respectful working relations. We still maintain good friendships with Ethiopians we met then.

When we arrived in Ethiopia, Haile Selassie was an old man whose empire was unraveling. Although the capital, Addis Ababa, was being modernized, most of the country had remained little changed for over a thousand years. There were severe droughts in parts of the country. Many people were starving while in other places food was plentiful.

The emperor took pride in the university he founded, Haile Selassie I University, and would attend graduation ceremonies, even bringing his little dog. I came to teach physics in this university and my wife taught mathematics in a Jesuit high school, Teferi Mekonnen, another of the emperor's names. Our daughter Jackie was seven years old and our son Dan, was four.

This was a time when the university students were impatient for real change and the situation was volatile. The four years we lived in Ethiopia were exciting but tragic times. We lived with the hope that wisdom would prevail. Unfortunately, within two years after our departure, the emperor was imprisoned, and the students victimized by a ruthless reign of terror. Many of our students were killed, imprisoned or became refugees from their country. Life in Ethiopia took a serious decline, and it took almost 20 years for Ethiopia to return to being a place like the country where my family and I lived, taught and studied.

CHAPTER 1
SETTLING IN

With our first look flying into Ethiopia, we knew we were entering a beautiful and fascinating country. In September the hills are green and lush with meadows of yellow Meskel flowers. To us, Ethiopia was a kingdom in a fairy tale; we knew little about it but were eager to explore. We had no idea of the adventures that lay ahead or the fascinating people we would be living and working with. Those experiences changed our lives forever.

First came all the tasks needed to begin life in a new place. We had purchased a VW camper in Europe and after a summer of touring, shipped it from Frankfurt. We naively thought that, if we stayed a few days in Athens, our car would greet us in Addis Ababa when we arrived. We were totally unaware of the relaxed speed of ocean shipping at that time and the thoroughness of Ethiopian customs agents. Although we arrived in early September, we did not see the car until late November and only then did the negotiations with customs begin. Luxury cars were taxed at 100% duty and a VW camper sure looked like a luxury car to them. Finally, we agreed to only tax the camping equipment as luxury and the van as a car. Even so, we knew Betty Lu would be working for a year just to pay this off.

Our daughter Jackie and son Danny needed schools and Betty Lu needed that job. The American school was priced out of reach. Only those with contracts that paid school expenses could afford it; my contract did not. Fortunately, there was a wonderful alternative for Jackie, Good Shepherd School. This was a school for children of missionaries but they also accepted others at a reasonable fee to help with the operating expenses. Danny was too young for Good Shepherd so he went to a private kindergarten, Jack and Jill and then later to the English School. Both schools had students from almost everywhere and our kids enjoyed these new interesting friends. The invitations to Danny's birthday party read like a page from a UN directory.

We had taken over an apartment from a departing Fulbright professor, fully furnished and he bequeathed us a very good cook. The apartment was in a good neighborhood with lots of expatriates. This was fortunate since we did not yet have our car and other expatriates were generous with rides. We all shared a common bond of living in a foreign land. Also, Addis had an incredible shared- taxi system. You stood on a corner and when a taxi came near, you yelled your destination. If he had room and was heading near there, he signaled and you jumped in. The fare was 50 cents if you were going uphill and 25 cents for a downhill trip. The US dollar equaled 8 birr, so uphill was about 6 US cents.

CHAPTER 2
ADDIS ABABA AND PLACES NEARBY

In 1969, Addis Ababa, the capital of Ethiopia, was an international city with people from all over the world. The UN had a large office there and so did the Organization of African Unity. Of course, all the embassies were there. At that time, the US had a large military presence called the Mapping Mission. This had little effect on us except for the movie theater that showed American movies. The most useful American presence was the United States Information Service (USIS) which we frequently used for books and films. USAID helped Ethiopia in agriculture and education. In addition, there were numbers of mission groups and NGO's from other countries. Many of these expatriates became an important part of our lives and, indeed, remained our friends long after leaving Ethiopia.

We were all foreigners living in a very unusual place. Ethiopia is an ancient Christian country, adopting Christianity as early as the 6th century. It was isolated by Muslim countries and therefore developed many distinct religious customs. The Ethiopian Orthodox church uses Ge'ez as a religious language and celebrates its own unique festivals. After arriving, we attended the Meskel Festival which celebrates the finding of the true cross by Emperor Constantine's mother. Foreigners were given special seating near the emperor, Haile Selassie. First, a tall pile of branches, about 50-feet high, was assembled. Then the action started with a procession of church leaders in colorful robes and floats, some with neon lights. When it was dark, the pile of wood was ignited and flames rushed upward. The parade made three trips around the fire and soon after, the burning wood tumbled down making a spectacular flare.

This was our first time to see the emperor, Haile Selassie. He was probably the last functioning emperor of Ethiopia. He maintained the traditions of emperors. He was dressed in a decorated military uniform and attended by his own elite security guards dressed in special green uniforms and driving green VW Beetles. A small man, sitting on a large throne. However, he was a man with almost unlimited power in his country and feared by all. The ordinary people revered him and that seemed to be his source of power. When he traveled, people would line the roads to receive gifts of sandwiches and white cloth tossed by his aides. They would cry out with strange chanting like yodeling. He was an astute politician, rotating those under him to keep them from developing a following and also maintaining that elaborate secret service.

The countryside was a different world, little changed since biblical times. Plowing is still done by oxen, and threshing by oxen trampling the grain stalks. Farmers tossed the stalks into the wind with forks to separate the grain from the straw. These small farms are almost self-sufficient, meeting the needs of the small family living there. The life of the farm families looked idyllic but in times of drought there was hunger and this happened all too often.

Addis Ababa sits on a 7000-foot-high plateau on the edge of the Rift Valley. While Addis is cool and moist, the valley is hot and dry. The Rift Valley near Addis is a fascinating place where we often visited. It contains the Awash River with hippos and crocodiles. Part of the river is in the Awash National Park, a wildlife reserve. Although it was home to a delightful variety of wildlife, it did not include the more dangerous animals such as the big cats, rhinos, elephants and buffalos. The reason was clear. Although a reserve, this place was home to a large number of people with guns and cattle.

Near the river is Sodere Hot Springs with a swimming pool, public baths and a hotel with a campground. Another hot springs farther away was totally undeveloped and far from any main road.

We called it Palm Springs since it was in a little oasis with palm trees. When student protests closed the schools, we spent many wonderful days in the Rift Valley. However, our favorite places were at the lakes. Each lake in the Rift Valley was different from the others. The first lake, Langano, appeared brown because of the pumice grains suspended in the water. The pumice did not affect the swimming except it had the strange effect of absorbing the sun's heat near the surface of the water. The surface was pleasantly warm but the water underneath was unpleasantly cold. We enjoyed swimming there: often floating on the warm surface. The next lake had no pumice but had hot springs that saturated the water with minerals. Water from the hot springs was too hot for swimming but wading could be nice when the hot water was mixed with the lake's cold water. Other lakes south in the valley were good for fishing but questionable for fear of bilharzia. We seldom went to those lakes but would buy fish from enterprising young entrepreneurs.

CHAPTER 3
HAILE SELASSIE THE FIRST UNIVERSITY

Although the university had several campuses around Addis, the two main ones were at Arat Kilo and Sidist Kilo. The names, translated into English, were four kilometers and six kilometers. The distance was from some reference which I assumed to be the emperor's palace. Arat Kilo housed the sciences including the physics department where I taught. At that time, our classes and labs were in what was once the emperor's stable. That may sound primitive, but the facilities were actually adequate. Sidist Kilo housed the liberal arts and social science departments as well as the University Administration buildings. The university administration was in former royal buildings with much more stature than our stables.

Only the fittest of students managed to attain university entrance. Starting as young children, tests would determine who could go on to the next level. Finally, the students needed to pass a university entrance examination. Although the students were clearly bright, they struggled in their freshman year. Understanding the variety of English accents and reading college level texts was a severe challenge. Most had grown up without access to books or spoken English.

The students loved their country and wanted it to modernize and develop politically and economically. They felt the emperor had been a positive force in the past but he was now too old and was holding the country back. Their only weapon was to protest. They did this by marching to gain public support, boycotting classes, publishing newspapers critical of the government and taking over a university coffee shop. These actions were destined to lead to a confrontation with the emperor's power; his secret service, bodyguards, police and army.

Betty Lu was teaching at an elite secondary administered by Jesuits. Her students shared the feelings of the university students and would protest when they felt the government was in the wrong, which was often.

CHAPTER 4
FIRST ACADEMIC YEAR

We settled into a life that was not much different from back home. Our apartment was modest but modern, with modern utilities and situated in the nice neighborhood of Casa Incis. There was such a large number of foreigners living in Addis Ababa that they, naturally, formed their own community. Since Americans were in the majority, American English and American ways were normal. Gradually over time, we developed Ethiopian friendships, but they did most of the adapting—speaking English and following Western customs.

Organizations that employed a significant number of foreigners, like the University, needed to use English as the working language and follow western customs. An interesting example is something as basic as time of day. In traditional Ethiopian time, the day starts at 6 am and the hours are numbered starting at zero (our 6 am is 0 in Ethiopia). A faculty meeting scheduled at 3:00 in Ethiopian time (9 am) would have been missed by Americans. Since Western time was used where we worked, most foreigners, including us, were not even aware there was Ethiopian time. Even though we were in an exotic place far from America, both at home and at work, we were mostly in a comfortable Western environment.

One Ethiopian custom we were quick to embrace was to enjoy Ethiopian coffee houses. Near the campus was the Jolly Bar, a coffee house far ahead of its time (think Starbucks). Their version of cappuccino, with cocoa floating on the top, was the best coffee drink I have ever had. The Jolly Bar is still there today but now it is an upscale nightclub.

Each weekday, the four of us needed to go in four separate directions. At first, Jackie went to a neighbor's house to catch the bus to her school, Good Shepherd. Since the bus stop was near the Emperor's Palace, it was quite safe. Roads were crowded with vehicles in poor condition and frequently overloaded. Accidents were common. The bus was not exempt. We got a call from the school that the bus had rolled over three times and some of the children were hurt. Still without a car, with difficulty we made our way to the few hospitals where Jackie might have been taken. We had a terrible few hours before we found Jackie was safe.

Dan was taken to Jack and Jill by our inherited male cook. One advantage in living in Africa was the low cost and availability of very good cooks and housekeepers. Later there was a parting of the ways and we, like most foreigners, employed a female housekeeper and cook. When we moved into a house, we employed a guard. These domestic workers were skilled and trustworthy and treated well by most of the foreign community.

Betty Lu took a shared taxi to Tafari Mekonnen high school to teach math and English. The school was very crowded and was forced to have two shifts. Betty Lu took a morning shift and so was home early to gather in the kids.

I caught a ride with a Dutch friend, Anton Van Putten, to the university at Arat Kilo. The Van Puttens were our neighbors and were very helpful to us. Most of our socializing this first year was with Europeans and other Americans. Since we were still without our car, one American family adopted us. They took us to church and even once on an excursion out of the city to Lake Langano.

The university academic system was a copy of those in the US so there was little adjustment needed. However, towards the end of the first semester, a few things happened showing us that Ethiopian students were far different from American students. The first occurred about the middle of November. A large number of students gathered on the Arat Kilo campus to demonstrate against the US involvement in the Vietnam War. There were speeches but no violent demonstrations so I went up to join them. At that time, I was also against the war. I was readily accepted even though I was obviously an American. I was told by students that they were against the US government actions and not Americans. The Ethiopian government did not take any action against this demonstration. Later, when the students marched off campus with their demonstrations, the government did take strong action. Education was highly valued by the students and their families. For the students to risk their education for demonstrations about a war that did not affect them, showed a strong desire to improve their country so it could play an important role in the world.

Student unrest also extended to the secondary schools. Betty Lu's school needed to use split shifts to accommodate all the students. The afternoon students felt they were suffering an injustice since they felt the morning students had some advantages. The afternoon students occupied the classrooms and would not leave. This forced the school to close until this was sorted out.

The second event was the first round of physics examinations. The students did very poorly. The Physics Department was mainly run by the foreign staff with PhDs, with only a few Ethiopian staff with MS degrees. We knew that the students had passed a series of examinations that passed only the top scorers. As a result, we had only the tip of a very steep pyramid of students. However, they did not do well on our exams. Slowly, students and staff adjusted to each other. Time was needed for the students to adjust to hearing spoken English, especially English in the many dialects spoken by the staff. Also, students did not have books in their homes, and it took time to learn how to handle academic textbooks. Finally, Ethiopian schools relied on memorization and did not stress the problem-solving skills needed for the study of physics. Eventually, the students did catch up, and many entered top American graduate schools and graduated with distinction. Several got PhDs in physics or engineering.

The third event involved a young Austrian man named Gerhart Klauda who I met walking on the street. As we walked together, he told me about his simple lifestyle and his passion for the poor who suffered from leprosy. He was running a project to employ them in a workshop making rugs and furniture. Leprosy had long plagued Ethiopia, crippling many people. Fortunately, a drug was available to arrest the disease, so the victims were no longer contagious. However, there remained a strong fear and prejudice against these people and most ended up begging.

When he found that I worked at the university, he asked me to help arrange for him to make a talk there. He wanted to recruit students to join him in fighting the prejudice towards leprosy victims so they could rejoin society. We arranged for Gerhart to speak before a free movie for the students. When the time came, we entered a large hall packed with noisy students. Gerhart started his talk, but the students began calling loudly for the movie. I wanted to leave, but Gerhart kept on. Slowly the students near him started to listen. Soon quiet spread to the entire room. The students related to the plight of the leprosy victims and at the end, many volunteered to help. Clearly, the students had experienced many hardships themselves that prepared them for the challenges of life and made them sensitive to the needs of others.

There was great excitement when we saw our car through the fence of the customs yard. We rushed in to get it, only to be halted by the customs agents. We had heard that Ethiopian custom agents are corrupt, unlike the American system. In this case, we found the agent to be a hard and persistent bargainer with no hint of dishonesty. In the end we found he was reasonable, extracting lots of needed revenue for his government but not leaving us destitute. Later when I tried to return to the US with some science equipment I borrowed from a US university, our customs system was so inflexible that the equipment had to be abandoned because I didn't have the proper documents. Anyway, we had our car and our lives were changed for both the good and bad. With a car, we could explore the fascinating cultural and scenic places of Ethiopia, isolated from the poverty and hassle encountered walking the streets. One American teacher who lived less than a block from the university, would drive to work to avoid harassment by the beggars on the street. The several months we spent walking streets provided a strong motivation for us to join others in trying to improve the lives of street people. It also made us comfortable walking the crowded streets in Africa. This served us well in the many years we were to live there.

With the arrival of the car came the freedom to experience the exciting places in the Rift Valley and mountains around Addis. The first trip was to Lake Langano followed quickly by a return to the Rift Valley to visit the Sodere Hot Springs. On that trip we traveled along the Awash River and saw small crocodiles. Nearby was a young boy washing in the river, without any fear of the crocodiles. Along the river a short distance away was the hippo pool. A muddy pond with hippos. Nobody swam there. We visited a sugar plantation with an ancient sugar mill. The sugar mill was like a working museum filled with old motors, pumps and boilers. Somehow the Dutch operators managed to keep the equipment operating.

The next trip was upward on Mt. Entoto, a small mountain just beside Addis. At the top is an old traditional Ethiopian church and a monastery. The church is in the traditional shape of a tukul with eight sides. Inside was a chamber where only the priests can go. Orthodox churches are modeled after the first Jewish temple in the Old Testament with a Holy of Holy where God is present. This chamber is considered sacred and contains a replica of the arc of Moses described in the Old Testament. In the arc is the Tabot, a plate or board on which the 10 commandments are inscribed. The monastery appeared to have both male priests and elderly women. The priests were memorizing scriptures, and the widows were doing domestic work.

CHAPTER 5
THE PEACE IS BROKEN

Until late in December, the student's demonstrations had been peaceful and the government's response restrained. Tension was high as the students continued to press their issues: to have a newspaper (free press), and be able to demonstrate off-campus, etc. Then, on December 30th, the president of the Student Council was shot and killed by someone. The killer escaped in a waiting car. No one knows who the killer was, but the students assumed he worked for the secret police. The students somehow got the body to Sidist Kilo and took it to the medical center there for examination. They were preparing for a march to take the body to the home of the parents. The police demanded the body and the military, heavily armed, entered the campus. Armed police or military on the campus was in violation of an informal agreement between the students and the government. Students from all over the city streamed to the Sidist Kilo campus until a large crowd was there. Even high school and elementary school students came. In this dangerous situation, someone fired a shot. Then the military opened fire killing and wounding several students. The official report was that 3 were killed and 5 wounded but the numbers were actually higher. One faculty member was shot in the foot. Fortunately, I was not at Sidist Kilo that day.

Students fled the campus; some returned to their homes. After this, the students refused to come to class. The faculty refused to teach until the government provided guarantees that armed soldiers would never again enter the campuses. The government ordered the university and high schools to be shut. So classes were stopped by the students, staff and the government. We were both under contract to teach, but we had a long time to wait before any classes would resume.

CHAPTER 6
TRAVEL IN ETHIOPIA

With our schools closed, we decided to visit some of the unique places in Ethiopia. Harar is an ancient Muslim city on the East side of the Rift Valley. It's a walled city that was off-limits to non-Muslims until recent times. Visiting there required crossing the Rift Valley. We stopped in the Awash Game Park and enjoyed seeing the Oryx, an animal both beautiful and impressive in size. Then we traveled to the city of Dire Dawa and met some American teachers from the physics department, the Gale's and Donner's. We camped in the parking lot of the Ras Hotel. Most of the towns in Ethiopia had a Ras Hotel which was often the center of nightlife. The next day, we all bundled into the camper and climbed the long hill up to Harar. It was just as exotic as we had heard. The gates and walls were impressive. Three bonuses for visitors were the colorful baskets they made, rides in a horse cart and the hyena man. This man would hand-feed the hyenas for a small fee. Hyenas are dangerous so the man had become famous. We camped in the parking lot of the Ras Hotel there also. It was the center of nightlife for that small and quiet city.

Heading back, we stopped at Alemaya University. This university, with its demonstration farm, was started by the University of Oklahoma with funding from the US government. It had the looks of an American college. The campus was beautifully situated on Lake Alemaya which is about 30 miles from Harar. Sadly, the lake disappeared when it was overused for irrigation and drinking water. We were thinking about transferring there to teach.

I did in fact return to teach there when Betty Lu got a position teaching English in Harrar, but that was over 30 years later.

Palm Springs was on the way back so we decided to camp there. It's very isolated, about 30 miles from the road. The spring had two pools, one very hot, like a hot tub, and one rather pleasantly warm. I swam in the hot pool and the kids swam in the warm one. Later that evening, as we watched the pools, a crocodile swam across the warm pool where the kids had been. We received another surprise the next morning when a young man from the local tribe showed up armed with a spear. He asked for a *caramello* (candy) which we didn't have. He then offered to sell us his spear which we gladly agreed to buy. We stopped again in Awash Game Park and Sodere, where we purchased a new pet, George the curious monkey.

Since our schools were still closed when we returned to Addis, we decided to make a trip in the other direction to Lake Tana. Our Dutch friends, the Van Puten's, traveled with us in their small car. The trip required crossing the Blue Nile Gorge which has a bad reputation for robberies. We took an Ethiopian friend, Hailu, with us and he carried a handgun. However, as we approached the gorge, he hid the gun under the seat. He did not want it to be stolen. We did not see any robbers. A bonus in crossing the gorge is the chance to see the Blue Nile Falls. It is a spectacular sight, rivaling Niagara Falls. The Blue Nile River flows into the White Nile and is the largest contributor to the Nile River.

Lake Tana is a very large lake which is the source of the Blue Nile. It has several islands with famous monasteries. Ethiopian tradition tells of taking the Arc of the Covenant from Jerusalem and bringing it to Axum in Ethiopia. During its long journey, it rested for many years on an island in Lake Tana. We rented a boat to take us to some of the islands. Betty Lu was not too happy to go since only men are allowed on the islands and she would have to remain on the boat. Anyway, we did not make it very far. We ran out of fuel and spent the two hours waiting in the boat for something to happen. Finally, a boat came along and picked us up. They took us to an island with an interesting church where the males could see the ancient crowns of Teodros and Yohannes, two important emperors of Ethiopia. There were a number of interesting churches around the lake. Many of these had walls covered with colorful paintings. These were opened to both men and women.

We then traveled north to Gondar, an ancient capital of Ethiopia. The Van Puten's radiator was being repaired, so we all squeezed into the camper. We saw the famous Debra Berhan Selassie church. The walls are covered with colorful cartoon-like paintings from Biblical and traditional stories and the ceiling is painted with angles looking down. Also, there is an impressive old castle with a famous pool known as the Bath of Fasilidas. This pool is the place where Muslims, newly converted to the Christian faith, were baptized. The next day was *Timket*, the day when thousands of Ethiopian Christians come to celebrate the baptism of Jesus by John the Baptist. This holiday and Meskel, are the premier religious holidays for Christians—not Christmas and Easter. Fortunately we left before the crowds came.

On our return trip to Addis, we found that much of the road had been graded with sharp crushed stones. Van Putten's car had 5 flat tires with two of the tires ruined. In addition, his radiator had to be repaired again. I had several flat tires and 2 ruined tires as well. Fortunately, there were lots of enterprising people along the road to fix tires but replacements for ruined VW camper van tires were not to be found. We ended up camping by the road and sending Hailu ahead by truck to get Grant Gale, to come and bring us a tire, money and food. Early the next day, we met a man in a VW Beetle who loaned us his spare tire. I was amazed that the beetle wheel fit on a VW camping van. With that, we limped along towards Addis until we met Grant with new tires and some food.

One trip, cut short, was very memorable. Grant Gale and I went with three students to visit a small isolated town in the more tropical south. We were invited by a teacher to stay with him and show some movies since the locals had nothing like that in their village. We borrowed a projector, generator, screen and some movies and headed out. We set up in a large field. Word spread and soon we were surrounded by a large mob of people, all trying to get close enough to see the movie. Unfortunately, they crowded into the space between the projector and the screen. It was dark and the crowd was getting angry. We had no way to elevate the projector or the screen. Even if we could, the crowd was just too big for all to see. We decided to pack up our equipment and make a run for it. As the VW pushed its way through the crowd, we heard thuds of something hitting the roof. Fortunately, the place lacked rocks so the angry people were throwing what they had, clods of earth. We got to the village just ahead of the people and drove the car into the gated-compound of the teacher. There we spend the night and slipped out of town early the next day.

George our monkey, aptly named for Curious George, was wearing out his welcome so we decided to take him for a ride. There are many monkeys like him at Sodere so we hoped he would like to join them. We camped there for the weekend. As soon as the other monkeys saw George, they chased him, he was not one of them. This chase was clearly not for fun but to kill a male invader. George wisely ran into the men's restrooms and stayed put. That night he came out and spent the night in a tree near us. We took him back to Addis the next day.

George caused a dangerous situation at our house although it was not his fault. Another monkey, bigger than George and wearing a collar, wandered into our yard to visit George. It bit Jackie. This raised the serious concern of rabies. Our only hope was to capture the monkey and take him in for testing. With great effort and a banana, we lured him into the house and then into a cage. The Pasteur Institute was active in Ethiopia at that time and they tested the monkey and kept it for research. The test was negative so we could go ahead with our summer plans.

Eventually, we decided George had to leave. Unfortunately, he had developed the habit of masturbating in public. With lots of little kids around, this was not a good thing. At this point, we had moved into a house by the French Embassy which was in a forest near Addis. We let him go in the forest. He was happy to get into the trees and we never saw him again.

CHAPTER 7
SUMMER TRAVEL TO KENYA

We had the summer free and decided to drive to Kenya. Driving from Ethiopia to Kenya was not easy since the roads are either very rough or not there at all. You must cross parts of Ethiopia and the Northern Frontier of Kenya where robbers were not uncommon. After a lot of discussion, we and two other families decided to caravan together. We selected a route. Others had taken this route and described its starting point as "go eight miles south of Neghelle and stand on the roof of your car. Look around until you see a track that you are certain could not be going to Kenya. That's the road". It is very dusty and very rough. We only made 40 miles the first day. At one point the track crosses a deep canyon on an ancient bridge. The structure was steel, but the roadbed was of rotted timbers. Only the driver, me, was in the car when it crossed. For a small fee, a villager would move the least rotten timbers from the back to the front of the car. Finally, near the other side, I simply dashed off the bridge. We decided not to return that way. However, not a robber was to be seen. We had prepared by taking jerry cans of fuel and water and several spare tires. We had an argument with customs at the border because we lacked an export-import permit for the car. Finally we crossed into Kenya. Our car was only a year old but engines wear out quickly on the dusty roads. We had no trouble this time, but two years later on the same trip, it was a different story.

Idi Amin was the new Ugandan President, and we had heard bad things about him. Uganda was a beautiful place at that time so we decided to go anyway, before the political situation worsened. First we stopped in Nairobi, the city of Dairy Queens, laundromats and straight streets. We camped in the city park, famous for its large trees laced with bougainvillea's. With all of our supplies renewed, we went to Murchison Falls National Park in Uganda. The elephants and buffalo were only 10 feet from the car. Then we took a small boat up the river to see the falls. The hippos and crocodiles surrounded the boat. All this was very exciting. We then went to Queen Elizabeth Park to see lions. Jackie was the first to find one sleeping under a tree, not so exciting.

At that time, East Africa had three main universities, Haile Selassie I University in Addis, the University of Nairobi in Kenya and Makerere University in Uganda. We visited Makerere and found it to be an established university with good facilities. We rated it a little better than our university in Addis. Many years later, after all the political upheavals, we returned to find the university only a hollow shell of its past.

Then we were off to Tanzania, to see the famous Ngorongoro Crater game park, with its lions, rhinoceros, wildebeests, and zebras. We visited Serengeti which was also famous for lions, cheetahs hyenas and giraffes. We just could not get enough of the excitement of seeing such magnificent animals in their natural world. We also realized that you do not really need a guide. You know there's an interesting animal near when you see several Land Rovers and minivans clustered together! Camping in a game park was much more relaxing in an enclosed VW camper than in a tent, though tents were there, too.

Next, we traveled East to the beautiful resort of Malindi, Kenya on the Indian Ocean. The coral and fish there were incredible, the beaches beautiful and the water warm. After a few wonderful days, we moved down the coast to Mombasa. An English man told us camping was not safe, and he invited us to park in his hotel parking lot. We went on and an Indian family on the beach also told us not to camp but to come to their place where it was safe. We ended up camping in their back yard near their watchman. The next day we moved to a safe campground with security guards. We went on to Dar es Salaam, Tanzania, but some friends there had had their car broken into so we moved inland to Kilimanjaro. We had no idea about the difficulties of climbing but when we asked we were refused. They said kids the size of ours would not be able to make the climb. Fortunately, we were rejected since we learned later the climb is long and hard. We moved on to Tsavo, with its huge herds of elephants. Eventually, it was time to return home for classes. On the way out of Kenya, we visited Lake Nakuru, with its beautiful pink flamingoes.

We returned to Addis a different way. This new route required climbing the Mega hill and this could be impassible if it was wet. We could see that much of the road was in black cotton soil, a soil type that becomes very sticky and slippery when wet. Luckily, when we arrived, the road was dry, and we had no trouble. There was an Italian fort in Mega and an old Italian stone road leading towards home. People had long ago abandoned the stone road and drove on the smoother dirt. We had no problems, not even a flat tire, and returned safely to Addis.

CHAPTER 8
SECOND ACADEMIC YEAR

Our lives changed in the second academic year. I became chairman of the Physics Department with many responsibilities within the department, the university and with high school education. A new American physics professor, Bob Fouchaux, came with his wife and family. Dan moved up to attend the English School. Betty Lu continued at Teferi Mekonen and Jackie stayed at Good Shepherd. We moved from Casa Inchis to a house on a road near the French Embassy.

The plight of the poor in Ethiopia became more and more of a burden to us. Every day we would encounter survivors of polio and leprosy begging in the streets. Every day we were stopped by street children asking for money or to shine shoes. Much of our time together with friends was spent in sharing our frustration at not being able to do anything. Finally a breakthrough came. We started attending the Presbyterian Church where Dave Philips was pastor and joined a small group that was studying Luke. Luke describes the setting where Jesus lived as similar to ours in Ethiopia. The poor were helpless widows and orphans. Jesus often emphasized his concern for the poor and his wishes for followers to share. This study added to our wish to do something about the beggars and street children.

In October, Betty Lu's parents and her aunt Mary Kaye came to visit. They bravely went around on the local taxis. We took them in our VW to visit the local high points, Mt. Entoto, Mt. Menagesha and the famous mercarto. The mercarto is famous for being the largest outdoor market in Africa and almost anything can be found there. Unfortunately, it is also famous for pickpockets, purse snatchers and young men who will guide and protect you for a fee. Down in the Rift Valley, they enjoyed the wildlife in Awash Game Park and we even visited Palm Springs.

Our good fortune in traveling was about to end. We traveled to Assab, now part of Eritrea, on the coast of the Red Sea with the Fouchaux family, Bob, Judy, two kids and three dogs. They had an old Jeep that had seen better days. The beaches on the Red Sea were beautiful and undeveloped. We camped on the beach and enjoyed fresh fish and lobster (crayfish) purchased at our camper door. The water was warm and clear and soon we found we were swimming with large manta rays. They certainly looked fearsome, but they were totally uninterested in us.

It was on the way back that the trouble started. We were well in the lead and stopped to let the Fouchauxs catch up. They failed to come so we went back. We saw their car smashed against rocks, about halfway down a steep part in the road. The brake fluid line had broken and without brakes on the hill, Bob had to choose between hitting the rocks or going over the edge of a cliff. Bob decided the rocks were best but by this time, he was moving fast. In the crash, he seriously smashed his arm resulting in badly broken bones. We loaded him into our car and returned to Assab. Bob was in great pain and the rough road was difficult for him. Finally back in Assab, we found there was only a small clinic and no way to treat the broken bones. We arranged for Bob and Judy to fly back to Addis and we took their two kids and three dogs with us to Addis in our car.

Ethiopia has some very inaccessible places. One of these is the Danikil Depression in the Rift Valley. The place contained several active volcanos but few people were willing to venture in to see them. The Danikil people who lived there were rumored to be a fearsome tribe. Their ritual of manhood for young men was to obtain the testicles of a man.

The geology department wanted to see the volcanos, so they decided the safest way was to rent a small plane to overfly the area.

They had room for one more and invited me, which was a mistake for them. The plane flew low so the geologists could see the landscape. Unfortunately, that made the flight very rough and I don't react well to motion. I became sick and set off a chain of events where each in turn threw up. Things could have been worse. About a week later, I saw the same plane sitting in a field. Apparently it had made an emergency landing.

We had purchased a half-interest in two horses. We alternated with our new friends, the Fouchaux, each keeping the horses for a month. Our time as horse owners was not destined to end well. At the end of each month, the horses needed to be moved between our home and the Fouchauxs. One time, one of Fouchaux's children Richard, and I, were riding the horses between our homes. We lived a few miles apart and needed to travel over some paved roads. It was threatening rain and we were in a hurry. My horse was spooked and started running. He crossed a paved road and slipped on the pavement. We went down with my leg under the horse. The weight of the horse and the impact with the pavement resulted in a broken ankle and a fractured kneecap. I was fortunately in shock and could not feel pain. One of the Emperor's bodyguards, with a green VW beetle, was driving by. He stopped and literally picked me up and put me in his back seat. Richard Fouchaux took the horses home and called Betty Lu. The emperor's bodyguard dropped me at the best hospital in Addis. I never saw him again. However, now I was out of shock and the pain was terrible.

We had a friend, Red Fisher, who was a well-established orthopedic surgeon in the US. He had decided to stop mending the bones of drunk drivers in the US and instead help the poor leprosy patients in Ethiopia. He performed surgery to remove the kneecap and attach the tendons above the cap to those from below. The whole leg was then put into a cast. Neither Red Fisher nor the hospital ever presented a bill for what they did. I recovered use of my leg but the doctor said I could never play professional sports. Of course, he was right. The horses soon found a new home in an orphanage for needy children.

The university and schools opened and then closed again. There were more student protests, and the government was unwilling to meet any student demands. Jackie got the mumps, I had my cast removed, then Danny got the mumps as well. One of Betty Lu's students was very bright but also very poor. We helped him financially so he could stay in school. We arranged for him to assist Gerhart during the summer in managing a workshop for handicapped people. Finally by July we were ready for our long summer vacation!

CHAPTER 9
HOME LEAVE AFTER TWO YEARS

There are many wonderful places to visit between Ethiopia and the US. We started with a week in Egypt. When we took the airport bus into town, we were dropped at the Hilton hotel. It was so hot outside, we could not bring ourselves to go looking for a cheap hotel, so into the Hilton we went to check the price. Much to our surprise, the prices were very low. It seems that Cairo was expecting to be bombed by Israel and so there were no tourists. The National Museum was sandbagged but, other than that, everything was fine.

The small number of tourists had its advantages and disadvantages. None of the major sites were crowded but all the vendors seemed to be focused on us. At the Pyramids, we finally gave in to a man offering camel rides. All but Jackie enjoyed the camel rides. She refused to get up on a camel. We tried to climb up one of the pyramids, but the stones blocks were too big. It is truly amazing that builders were able to move them, and make such high structures!

On we went to Amsterdam, the city of flowers, cheese and windmills. After five days in Amsterdam, we headed back to the USA. We enjoyed the chance to visit our parents and families and friends, three weeks with each family. Our kids were spoiled by their grandparents.

On the return, we toured Cyprus and Israel. In Cyprus, we found that the island was divided into Greek and Turkish parts. The boundary was marked by piles of old oil barrels and patrolled by UN troops. We started on the Greek side in the King George Hotel. This was nice but too expensive so we moved to the Turkish side. The UN guards were certainly relaxed, but there was tension on the Turkish side. We traveled in a Turkish taxis but once got into a Greek bus. We found we were being escorted by heavily armed UN soldiers. The bus we were on was stopped and one man hauled off against his wishes.

The visit to Israel had to follow the visit to Egypt. To get the visa for Egypt, we could not have stamps from Israel in our passports. We loved Jerusalem and enjoyed wandering the narrow streets. It seemed so peaceful, we were able to visit Jericho, go into caves in the area where the Dead Sea Scrolls were found, and swim in the Dead Sea.

CHAPTER 10
THIRD ACADEMIC YEAR

The new academic year started with a new contract that covered school fees so we could afford to send both kids to Good Shepherd. They loved it there and Dan blossomed into a straight A student. We liked our new home, but it was rather remote and we felt the need for a guard dog. We got a German shepherd that was the product of an incestuous relationship. He seemed harmless until Jackie invited a number of friends over for a birthday party. The dog leapt for the throat of one girl. He scared her but didn't hurt her. Later, a goat passed near our open gate and the dog chased it and his owner. We could see them running over distant hills. The dog was returned by the goat's owner with a bill for the goat. It was time for a parting of the ways. Many places wanted a guard dog and did not care about his aggressive behavior or his moral character.

We continued to be concerned about the large number of beggars on the streets. Some adults could work but had been disfigured by leprosy. Even though they had taken medicine that arrested the disease and were not contagious, people were afraid and would not employ them. Gerhart Klauda, the one who spoke to the students about leprosy, had already set up a workshop where leprosy patients could work making wool rugs for sale (mainly) to expatriates. He had a plan to help more people. We would get the government to give us some land and resettle these beggars out there. Most had come from farms and would be happy to go. He put us on his committee to help organize this project.

Gerhart was a great visionary and fund raiser but had little skill for organization. He compensated for this with his recruitment skills. He put together a very hard working committee to help carry out the project. He raised enough funds to cover the costs for the first year. Everything was done but we still had not received any land from the government. We did not give up but continued to look for a way past the decision makers who were delaying us. Somehow, Gerhart convinced the Princess Mariam Senna to join our effort. We visited her library, filled with books in English and French. She was elegant and well-educated and spoke to us in perfect English. We were at a loss to know how to address a princess, but she put us at ease. Her participation in our project helped a lot. When she made requests, the government suddenly started to move. Soon we had our land. We went with the princess out to see the land. Getting this project started would eventually take a lot of time.

My position as Physics Department head required that I also assist in high school physics programs. When students finished high school, they had to pass the Ethiopian School Leaving Certificate Examination to enter the university. I helped in preparation and later I organized grading of the exams. In addition, I was an advisor on the high school curriculum. The most interesting thing I did related to high school was to visit classes being taught by our students between their third and fourth years. During that year, they were assigned to teach in remote high schools. I flew to Gambella, a small town near the Sudan border. When I arrived in the town I was met by the university students being escorted out of town by the police. The school was closed and the director was in hiding. Apparently the teachers (the university students), had roused the students on some issue and they stoned the director's house. Without the director, teachers or students, there was little I could do there. I then flew 15 minutes to another town, Pokwo, even more remote. I met a German driver there who had driven a car from Gambella to Pokwo and he told me that it took him 28 hours.

In Pokwo I visited a small Presbyterian mission with only 5 missionary families. It seemed that time had passed them by. One man had been a farmer in Nebraska. After three crop failures in a row, he felt God was calling him to be a missionary. In the center of the five mission homes was a beautiful little church shaped like a tukul. Drums were used in the service. The missionaries had helped villagers with raising chickens and gardening. When they tried to get them to use better gardening tools, they left them in the field at the end of a day. When one of the Ethiopian members was given a piece of clothing, it would often show up worn by another member in a few days, and gradually migrate around. They had no desire to own anything. They were a culture very different from ours with no sense of "private property." Unfortunately, the Presbyterian Church was having funding problems and was about to cut back their work there.

CHAPTER 11
SOF OMAR AND BALE NATIONAL PARK

We had heard stories about a stream and a cave cut by the water through a mountain. Within the mountain, there were beautifully carved passages and pools of water with blind fish and bats. We teamed up with the Fouchaux family, Bob now healed and with a new car and Mike Dante who had two boys staying with him. To prepare, we gathered information on the cave and borrowed helmets with carbide lamps from the Geology Department. After a long drive on bad roads, we reached a flat area near the cave entrance. A man with a rifle approached us and said this is a dangerous area and we should hire him to guard the cars. Since he had a rifle, it seemed like the only thing to do. He was probably right about the danger. We were in lands near the disputed border with Somalia.

From what we could see in daylight, the cave entrance and the stream entering the cave was manageable. The water was clean, a few feet deep but not flowing too fast. The next morning we entered the cave with our carbide lamps and some flashlights for backup. Our rough map was useless since there were many side passages and no obvious markers. Some of the stream crossings were deep, up to our necks. After many dead-end passages, we finally saw a faint light in the distance. Following that passage we found the end of the cave. We had passed through a ridge about a half-mile wide. Before us was a beautiful deep pool, ideal for swimming. It was only later that we found a sign warning about the crocodile that lived in the pool.

Richard Fouchaux, Danny and I decided to go back through the cave going against the stream. The rest hiked back over the ridge. The trip in the cave was uneventful except for one crossing. I was carrying Danny over a stream crossing. I badly misjudged the depth of the water and I found myself over my head and drifting into the blackness of an unexplored passage. I pushed Danny towards the shore and told him to swim for it. I did the same and somehow we both arrived there with our carbide lamps still burning. We continued through the cave and were all reunited at the cave entrance. Our cars and armed guard were still there. Only later did we have time to think about all the terrible things that could have happened to us.

On our way back, we spent some time at the Bale National Park. A family from Belgium attempted to raise sheep here. They built a large home out of the native stone which is quite beautiful. The area is very high, over 10,000 feet and cold at night. The government decided to make it a park and Peace Corp volunteers lived in the house and operated it as a park concession.

The park is home to a very rare antelope called the Nyala. By rising very early and going out with a volunteer, we were fortunate enough to see this elusive animal. There was a mountain stream in the park which had been stocked with trout long ago. The volunteers loaned us fly rods and I tried my luck. I caught three of the largest trout I have ever caught. On a fly rod, this was very exciting.

CHAPTER 12
PROBLEMS AT HOME
AND IN THE PHYSICS DEPARTMENT

Life continued but with a few problems. Jackie acquired some white rats, but they died. I think they were in the sun too long one day. Dan and the principal's son seemed to have teamed together to become the school terrors. Rich Whipple, the Dean of the Faculty of Science, was replaced by an Ethiopian. Rich was the person who hired me and we were friends, so it was an adjustment for me to lose him. He went off to study baboon social behavior, a hobby of his. I did not know at the time that he had a serious problem with alcohol. Later, I helped him to find a job where I was working but he eventually died of liver failure. Finally, and most serious, was that Betty Lu had a breast infection. An x-ray showed a suspicious spot, and a biopsy was taken. I was away from home at the time, visiting student teachers. She was taken to the hospital for a biopsy and a friend took care of the children. When I came home, the house was empty with neither wife nor children. Finally, after some frantic searching I found out what had happened. Fortunately, the biopsy showed that the spot was benign.

Don Meyer, one of the American physics professors in my department, was arrested by the police. He and a chemistry professor, Harry Unger, were illegally manufacturing LSD. Apparently the police found out about this when they were importing the chemicals. The police watched them to see who else was involved. When they starting selling the LSD to Ethiopians, the police pounced. After three weeks in prison, Don was not in very good shape. He was finally out on bail and eventually expelled. That wasn't the last time we saw him. A few months later, we were visiting the remote island of Lamu, off the coast of Kenya. Lamu was a beautiful paradise loved by the counterculture. In a coffee shop we met both Don and the chemistry teacher. Don was trying to get a job teaching in the local high school. Since he has a PhD from a highly regarded school, I wrote him a recommendation. Years later, I met him again in a hotel in Washington DC. I was attending a science fair where Danny had a successful entry and Don was presenting a paper in a meeting on the next floor. He still could not get free of drugs. That was the last time we met.

CHAPTER 13
THE RESETTLEMENT PROJECT

Many things happened quickly that had a strong influence on our remaining time in Ethiopia. First was the recruitment of a young carpenter from Austria to operate the resettlement site. His name is Bruno Thaler. He would prove to be one of the most capable men I have known. At that time we knew he was certainly a brave young man since he had barely come to Ethiopia and had no knowledge of the language or culture. With the aid of a university professor of social work, we selected our future settlers. After some training in house building, we purchased enough supplies for a week or two and rented a truck. Bruno, a traveler who offered to help, Mr. Czakany from Hungary, the settlers, wives and kids and a few animals headed off to the land. Nothing was well organized and apparently, the first night was horrible. The next day, some cooking was organized and some temporary shelters constructed. I expect if transportation was available, many would have given up and returned to Addis. In the long term, this experience set the correct tone. The settlers realized we barely knew what we were doing, and that they needed to look after themselves.

We needed to quickly plow the ground to put in the crops before the rains began. The ground was covered with grass that had not been plowed for centuries, if ever. We tried a rented tractor but it was not strong enough. Abebe, the chairman of our committee, and I went out to survey the situation. We realized we needed the most powerful tractor we could get. Finally after an emergency meeting of the committee back in Addis, we purchased a 75hp Italian tractor, the strongest available at that time. Since I grew up on a farm, I helped plow the first 18 hectares and then 10 to 15 hectares later were added later. Our first crop was Noug, an edible oil plant. It was supposed to kill the grass and add nitrogen to the soil. It seemed to work, but it grew so tall that the winds flattened much of it. Betty Lu was the car driver, purchaser and bookkeeper. Our kids loved the Site, as we called it. They loved Bruno, since he let them play with the animals.

Operating the Site was not easy. We secured another Austrian volunteer, Mr. Dorner, and he did far more harm than good. We never learned his first name. He totaled our pickup by hauling a heavy grain mill that he had been told not to purchase. He pulled up the corn our settlers had planted because he wanted to interplant with another crop. We had inherited an old dog that did nothing but sleep and eat. However, when Mr. Dorner would come near him, he would bark furiously. Apparently, he was an excellent judge of people. I wish we could have had that dog on our hiring committee.

We got a report that a woman settler had died and a man had his foot crushed. Most of the settlers had recovered from leprosy but had lost feeling to the feet and hands. As a result, injuries were common. However, this report was not totally correct. The woman did not die after all and the man's foot was damaged but no bones were broken. We got another report that one of the settlers was aggressive and threatened to kill Bruno. I went out with another board member to remove the man and return him to Addis. We put a shotgun under the seat to have if needed. The confrontation with the man lasted most of one day. We finally agreed to pay him to leave the site. That was safer than using the gun.

Since Bruno had no one to speak with in his native language of German, he quickly learned the two Ethiopian languages spoken there and his English also improved. He even managed to get his girlfriend in Austria to come out. She showed up at our house in Addis and said "This is Elizabeth". That was all the English she knew. Somehow she had flown to Ethiopia and gotten a taxi to our house. She was a nurse and with the two of them out there, things went much better. Much to our pleasure, eventually a catholic priest was passing by and he married them.

CHAPTER 14
MOVE TO THE BIG HOUSE

At the same time all of this was happening, Jack Smith, a long-time Presbyterian missionary, had to leave due to funding problems. He and his wife Evangel, had started a school for street boys in buildings behind their large, old house-(actually the former Italian Embassy) near the university. We were in a small study group with people concerned about the poor in Ethiopia. Dave Philips, the pastor of the Presbyterian Church, and his wife Kathy, were also in the group. We and the Philips decided to move into the old house and run the school, at least for the next year. This house did not come empty. The downstairs was also a hostel for protestant boys attending the university. Two of these boys, Negash and Abraham, grew up to be leaders in protestant churches and in education in Ethiopia. Another, Melkamu was successful in business and owned a nice home in Zimbabwe. Moges, Betty Lu's student whom we had been helping with school fees, also moved in. We also had Father Terry Moore, a priest who appeared to have been exiled to Ethiopia. Lastly, we inherited Rasu, the old dog with a passionate dislike for Mr. Dorner. Our house also became a Mecca for young adventurers from Europe. We would give them a meal, medications for their aliments and send them on their way. On their way out, they would tell incomers about our wonderful place. We enjoyed meeting these fascinating people. Our kids enjoyed living with three of their friends, the children of the Philips family, two girls in one room and three boys in another. What could be better than that?

Another group that sometimes showed up at the door were the blind students. Jack and Evangel had helped them start a musical group that would perform and receive donations. Betty Lu took over Evangel's job, looking for private schools, churches and other places they could perform.

CHAPTER 15
VISITORS FROM HOME

Traveling in Ethiopia had never been easy but it was always rewarding. We invited some friends of Betty Lu's parents to come to Ethiopia and travel some with us. They were an older couple but adventurous. We took them down into the Rift Valley to see Sodere and the animals along the Awash River. We had a good day and were headed back to Addis, just passing through the small town of Debra Zeit. In the rearview mirror, I saw a truck hit a man on a motorbike. We went back to check on the man and he seemed badly hurt. No one there seemed willing or able to help the man, so with the truck driver's help, we loaded the man onto the bed of the camper. There is a hospital in Debra Zeit so we took him there. Before he could be admitted, the police had to be called and a paper needed to be filled out. The man was eventually given medical care and so we started to leave. The police would not let us go. We had heard stories of foreigners being blamed for an accident and then money extorted from them. It was getting late and so we had a consultation with our friends and decided to make an escape plan. Our plan was to all quickly get into the car and make a run for it. The police did not have a car. Our friends would fake an illness if we were stopped. All started well but before we could get out of the gate, a guard at the gate had closed it. Our friends were crying out in faked pain. In the chaos I noticed that the gate did not have a lock. I slowly drove the car through the closed gate, pushing it open. The guard got out of the way and off we went. It all seems a little comical now, but at the time we were all frightened. Ever since that time, I never drove through Debra Zeit without worrying that a police car would pull us over.

CHAPTER 16
SECOND TRIP TO KENYA

The long summer break was upon us and it was time for our return to Kenya. We again made all the careful preparations. One thing was different however. Our car had endured two years of travel under rough, even brutal road conditions. We traveled alone part of this trip, perhaps a little overconfident. The Ethiopian part went well and on the border we camped next to a military outpost, parking just under a heavy gun. We now faced the Northern Frontier of Kenya, a dangerous, rough and dusty road. Our destination that day was Marsabit. Marsabit is a town on a mountain in the middle of this massive dry plain called the Northern Frontier. At the top of the mountain is a crater lake. It was said to be the home of a very old male elephant.

About half-way to Marsibit, the engine started missing and making some worrying sounds. I tried all the repair tricks I knew from many years as a VW owner. Finally the engine just froze up and stopped. I looked at the oil and could see flecks of aluminum in it. This meant the engine could not be repaired but needed to be replaced. It was getting dark but we could not move. We had no choice but to camp there on the road. Early the next morning, a large highway truck came by. The driver had a long rope and offered to tow us all the way to Marsabit, about 25 miles. That trip was frightening. Even with the long rope, the dust was so bad that we could hardly see even a few feet in front of us. The truck did not make any abrupt stops so we survived.

Marsabit is a small isolated place and there was only one person who had a truck that could haul our car. He was an Indian trader and, at that time, Kenya was trying to get rid of all the Indian traders. They had therefore canceled this man's business license. Over a beer, which I didn't like but drank to be social, we decided I would pay him an outrageous fee ($200) and he would transport us to Nairobi at night to avoid the police. Considering our total lack of options, the fee seemed like a bargain to me. The next day, with the help of the gathering crowd, we pushed the camper into the truck. The owner could not leave just then so he gave us a tour of the Game Park and the Crater Lake at the top of the mountain. He invited us to dinner as well. We started the next afternoon in order to arrive near Nairobi at night. In the daytime, the Northern Frontier is almost completely empty with little or no law enforcement. The only people we met were a group of professional guides with lion hunters. We traveled through the night and early in the morning ended up in a repair garage in Nairobi. We had traveled 400 miles in 15 hours.

The repair garage was, of course, owned by Indians. They agreed to replace my engine with a new one ($800) and grind off the new engine's serial number and stamp in my old one. This was needed to get back into Ethiopia without again paying a duty of 100%. The new engine was great but the work on the serial number was rather primitive. When we finally went through customs at the Ethiopian border, the customs agent laughed when he saw it. He was in a good mood and waved us through.

After the truck ride and new engine, we were almost completely out of money. We arranged for Betty Lu's parents to send money for us to a branch bank on the Kenya coast near Mombasa. We went there with only enough money for some simple food, mostly potatoes and eggs. Fortunately, we met a missionary family we knew in Ethiopia and they bought us some meals. Finally, the money came and off we went for another adventure.

In Ethiopia before coming to Kenya, we had met an interesting self-appointed missionary from Hungary who was working with the Masai tribe in Kenya, Mr. Czakany. He had been traveling through Addis and had decided to spend a few months helping us on the resettlement project. He had been with Bruno and the settlers for that first terrible night at the site. He had invited us to visit his work in Kenya so we visited the small village where he worked. The village was a collection of small huts shaped like domes with only an opening for a door. They had fires inside the huts that caused a lot of smoke and soot. The inside was indeed a foul place but I expect the smoke repelled mosquitos. Mr. Czakany's project was to install metal smoke stacks in the top of the dome houses to improve the air inside. This village seemed to have a lot of young Masai men with painted faces and spears. Some of the young men were very interested in Betty Lu's fine hair and one was interested in my watch. We thought it was time to leave, so we started off towards the car. One woman chased us trying to give us a drink of fermented milk and cow urine--most likely trying to be very welcoming. We politely refused and got out of there. We never saw Mr. Czakany again. We heard that he later drowned trying to rescue someone.

We ventured up the coast to Malindi, a place we had enjoyed two years earlier. The beauty of the beach had faded some, but it was a good jumping-off point for the Island of Lamu. The town of Lamu is an old Arab trading port and the island is an isolated paradise known only to a few. No cars are allowed on the island; the only entry is by a small boat. Our kids could run free since without cars it seemed to be a safe place. We gave them a little money and they came back with more delicious samosas than we could eat. The beaches were a fine white sand that I have not seen anywhere else. Dunes of the sand extended inland, forming private places for picnicking. The water was warm and crystal clear. Hotels and places to eat were very simple. The New Star Café had a simple menu but if you came late for any meal time, little was left. We ran into our friend, Don Meyer the LSD manufacturer. In every paradise, there is some problem. I did tangle with a Portuguese Man-of-War which was painful.

Back on the mainland, we camped in the Amboseli Game Park. The camp ground was an undeveloped clearing in the bush. Several families were bravely camped in tents around the clearing. Towards evening, several people were in the clearing gathering firewood when 10 hunting lions appeared. It looked like the people in the clearing were trapped. The lions ignored them and eventually moved on. I was very happy that we were inside our camper the whole time and did not need to go outside to rescue anyone.

On our trip back to Ethiopia, we joined up with a friend from the university with a nice Land Rover. Nothing went wrong other than the usual three flat tires. Before leaving Kenya, we purchased a little pet at Murchison Falls. It was a Jackson Chameleon. Later, we picked up a young hitchhiker going to Ethiopia who was a biologist interested in chameleons. He told us she was pregnant and would lay eggs. This was only partly true. She gave birth to 10 live babies while we were stopped at Lake Langano, almost home. Our hitchhiking guest said the mother does not care for them so they need to hunt on their own. He showed us how to feed them by putting them on a fingertip and pointing the finger towards a fly. Their long coiled tongue flicks out and the fly is suddenly in the mouth. We gave most away and only kept three; but it still required catching 35 flies every day. Later at home, in a large fishbowl, the mother had a second batch with no additional contact with a male. Not only did she not feed them, we found them disappearing one by one until only a few were left. Then we saw her eat one of her babies: nature's way of population control.

CHAPTER 17
FOURTH ACADEMIC YEAR

When we arrived at our house, we found a new guest. The Ethiopian head of our resettlement project, Abebe Haile, was moving to the US. He sent his wife ahead and he and his kids moved in with us. It was a very big house. He moved to a small town in Pennsylvania and later we have enjoyed several pleasant visits there.

Against my better judgement, I went on another trip with the Geology Department. In the air, I was the first to get airsick and all the others followed me one by one. I think this trip was their way to get even with me. This time we traveled to a remote high-elevation canyon. We arrived late with only some stale injera to eat. That night all our water froze. There was only more stale injera to eat for breakfast. Hiking down the canyon, I eventually became exhausted trying to keep up and turned back. Before long, I was out of water. Then the baboons on the cliffs above me starting dropping stones at me. These were stones weighing several pounds. Fortunately, they missed. Later I found that I may have been the first to observe such aggressive and intelligent behavior in baboons. Just before the steep climb out, I found a tiny spring of water and drank what I could. Then I climbed out. It was my last geology field trip in Ethiopia. After we left Ethiopia, I heard that one of my traveling companions was shot and killed at a security checkpoint. Bob Fouchaux was also shot at a security checkpoint but not killed.

A much more pleasant trip with the family was to the Bale Valley. This is a private valley only reachable by hiking about 2000 feet down. Some English expatriates rented the land and made it into a private resort, even with a swimming pool. It was a beautiful place even with the 2000 foot climb out.

We returned to the Bale Mountains for a packing trip together with our old friends the Fouchauxs and Dantes. Jackie did not feel well when we reached the lodge so she and Betty Lu stayed put while the rest of us ventured forth. We rented some horses and some lightweight sleeping bags. Because of the 12,000-foot elevation, there was little vegetation but what we saw was very strange. We had both a pack horse and a riding horse. After my past misadventures in riding, I walked. I will never forget the one night camping in a thin tent without warm sleeping bags. I was never so cold in my life. I tried doing exercises in the bag and that only caused perspiration that made the bag even less warm. We would have loved to explore the park more, but we needed much warmer gear.

CHAPTER 18
START OF HOPE ENTERPRISES IN ETHIOPIA

Jack Smith returned to work full time on the school for street boys. He had secured funding from World Vision and could expand the program beyond the children living in our place. At that time, street children were everywhere in Addis so the need was great. They shined shoes, guarded parked cars, sold gum or did whatever they could to get enough to eat. The street children lacked family support, many had come to Addis to seek their fortune. With enough funding for 400 boys, Jack expanded to a bigger location. That was only the beginning. The program grew to include girls, a trade school for teaching working skills and feeding programs for the very poor. When the political situation in Ethiopia became too dangerous for Jack to stay, he handed the program over to Dr. Minas. Dr. Minas was an Ethiopian who had studied in the US but bravely returned to help people in his own country. Hope continued to grow to include six primary and secondary schools throughout the country.

In recent times, a university was founded by Dr. Minas. We returned to Ethiopia for a few years to help get the university started. To this day, Jack's picture looks down on all of us passing through the Hope office in Addis. Jack Smith died in middle age from an undiagnosed disease, perhaps something he picked up working as a missionary in remote parts of Ethiopia. Jack Smith, his wife Evangel and Dr. Minas were truly inspiring people and we feel fortunate to have worked with them.

CHAPTER 19
WINDING DOWN

With only a few months left in Ethiopia, we were finishing up loose ends and coasting a little. Jackie got typhoid fever and lived in isolation for a few weeks. The police came into Betty Lu's school chasing students. When the students came into her classroom, she tried to defend them. A policeman kicked her and started beating the students. A senior officer came in and stopped them. Jackie was in a play called JB. She did very well but was killed at the end of the play. That did not seem to bother her but it did me. Betty Lu found a good tennis teacher and was taking lessons. We played at the US Embassy and she taught me what she learned. After living for almost four years in Ethiopia, all of this seemed almost like a routine normal life.

The resettlement project was actually doing fairly well. Homes had been built from Eucalyptus poles and chika (mud, straw, and cow manure). They had metal pan roofs and were quite comfortable. The main avenue was named after me. This was a once-in-a-lifetime honor and I really appreciated it. Unfortunately, that main street does not exist anymore. Bruno and Elizabeth lived closer to the road on the edge of a hill. A large barn was constructed there out of salvaged metal roofing and the animals were kept there.

Bruno and Elizabeth were managing the site very well. They would come to Addis every few weeks for supplies. One time Bruno came to a bible study high on something. We forgave him for that. After a lot of soul searching, we send Mr. Dorner back to

Austria. Mogus, Betty Lu's best student, spent the summer working at the site. This took courage since Ethiopians have a deep seated fear of leprosy. He later became a medical doctor and continued some contact with the settlers. Recently, he found us on the internet and we visited him in the US where he now lives and works as a medical doctor.

The final semester went very fast. All the time we had missed with student demonstrations and government shutdowns had to be made up. We managed to catch up and the final exams went off on schedule. I was pleased that many of the students did well and would provide the foundation for physics in Ethiopia.

Finally, we were dreaming of our trip home. Since I hadn't had any luck finding a position in the US, we were making big plans for a long, drawn-out trip. We planned to spend a week in Athens and Istanbul and then stay with some of the supporters of the resettlement project that live in Austria. After that, we would go to Sweden and Denmark; crossing over to Eastern Europe. Our ultimate goal was the Yugoslavian coast where we intended to camp out until it got cold. Then it would be back to the US to find a real job.

EPILOGUE

Two years after we left came the "creeping coup" against Haile Selassie. First he was under house arrest, then in prison and then probably killed. The coup was not let by the students but by low ranking military staff. The coup did not bring freedoms and human rights but instead, a brutal regime that imprisoned and executed many of the students. Some of the physics students and staff were in the US for graduate studies and they escaped, seeking asylum. The ones not so fortunate spent several years in prison. In fact, there were so many university students and professors in prison that they started a university inside the prison. Each person would teach a subject they knew and study the ones they did not know. One of the graduate staff when I was heading the physics department, Mulugeta, told me his story. His father was a governor and was executed when the coup happened. Mulugeta joined the student movement and was found out. He fled but was captured before leaving Ethiopia. He expected to be executed, but as the days of confinement continued his name was not called. Finally, he felt confident enough to start teaching a physics class. Another physicist, Negash, was in prison for his Christian beliefs. They wrote a physics textbook using all the scrapes of paper they could find. Later, Mulugeta became the Head of the Physics Department at the National University; the position I had when the National University was Haile Selassie the First University. Negash became President of a seminary and is now Dean of the Faculty of Science at Hope College.

With the overthrow of Haile Selassie followed by the chaotic conditions and the brutality of the new government, we assumed the resettlement project would have failed. All foreign help would have stopped. Volunteers and aid workers had to leave and no funding was coming to support the people. We heard second-hand rumors that the people were still there but we doubted the rumors could be true.

After 13 years, we were working in Zambia and visited Addis on our way home. We were curious about the fate of the people and wanted to visit the site and find what had happened to them. Abraham, the former student who lived with us in the old house, arranged transportation and guided us out of Addis to the site. The military government was still in power so it was illegal for foreigners to travel. If stopped, the danger would be for Abraham, not us. We would simply be booted from the country.

When we arrived near the site, we were shocked at what we saw. Off in the distance, were large piles of teff straw, evidence of a good harvest. This is a sure sign of prosperity in the Ethiopian countryside. Soon on the hillside, where the staff house and barn had been, we saw this prosperous village. Homes were neat and comfortable and there was a proper well and a grinding mill. Some women came out to see who we were. When they recognized us, they were so happy to see us. The men were out in the fields working but a few older men were there who remembered us. We had brought some soccer balls as gifts and when they hit the ground, about 60 healthy and well-dressed kids came out to play. One of the original settlers, an older lady, fell on the ground and hugged and kissed my feet. It was a very moving time for all of us; a moment to be treasured and remembered into old age.

They told us their story. With the chaotic situation when the new government took over, all the foreign support stopped and they were on their own. Their neighbors were threatening to make them leave because of prejudice about leprosy. Somehow they got some help from the local government. They were allowed to stay and were given some nice land near the original staff house where they could build a new village. The old village with Mr. Holland Avenue, returned to farm land. An aid organization gave them a grinding mill as a means for the village to earn some money. All the children are in school and not one has leprosy.

We were fortunate to be involved in carrying out the project, but the person who had the vision, raised the initial funds, and attracted the volunteers was Gerhart Klauda. It was the intensity of Gerhart Klauda's concern for the poor that attracted many of us to help in the projects he started. He gave all he could and took little care for himself. He slept on his desk and hitchhiked everywhere. Those of us inspired by him, took care of him, providing rides, meals and medical care. However, many of the people who support him, including us, left Ethiopia as our tours finished and others left as the political situation deteriorated. Gerhart's health began to decline and some of the needy people demanded more than he could give. Some claimed he was not distributing money given for them. We were not there and do not know firsthand the causes but Gerhart took his own life.

This repressive government continued for 18 years. After that time, Ethiopia was almost exactly where it had been when we left. Eighteen years had been wasted and some of Ethiopia's best people were either dead or in exile. At present, Ethiopia is still not a democracy nor does it stand very high on the human rights scale. However, the leadership has been stable and the country has progressed economically. People are living much better than in the time of Halie Selassie. Ethiopia is finally doing well.

Haile Selassie

The farms we saw were small and plowed by oxen

Prologue: Transport to the city markets was done by donkeys.

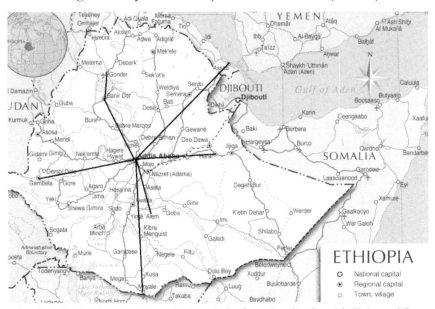

Settling In: This map shows Ethiopia before the divide with Eritrea. The lines indicate places we visited.

Addis Ababa and Places Nearby: Tectonic movement created the Rift Valley through the heart of Ethiopia and produces land at elevations of 7000 ft on both sides. I flew over a section of the Rift Valley where the thin crust causes several active volcanoes.

Addis Ababa and Places Nearby: The Meskel Festival is both beautiful and spectacular. It features religious dignitaries of all types in their beautiful robes, important leaders including Haile Selassie. The burning of the tall pile of timber provides a spectacular close.

Addis Ababa and Places Nearby: Without a car, we shopped locally with rare trips to the supermarket.

Haile Selassie the First University: Haile Selassie was very generous to education, donating property for the Mathematics and Physics Department where I worked.

Travel in Ethiopia: Isolated in the Rift Valley was a small hot spring called Palm Springs. There was nothing there but a beautiful Oasis.

Travel in Ethiopia: Gondar is a historic town that once was the capitol of Ethiopia.

Travel in Ethiopia: There were no maintained roads to Kenya, only the remains of roads from the Italian occupation. We crossed this bridge in our VW Camper.

Travel in Ethiopia: On the return from a trip to Red Sea beaches in the Rift Valley, Bob Fouchaux lost breaking on a steep cliff face. He saved the life of his family by steering into the rocks, but his arm was crushed.

Travel in Ethiopia: Near that time, I had a horse fall, crushing my leg. Red Fisher, a mission Orthopedic Surgeon was a friend and he patched up both myself and Bob.

Travel in Ethiopia: Sofo Omar Cave formed when a stream eroded a cave under a small mountain. We borrowed cave exploring equipment from Geology and I acquired an old map.

Travel in Ethiopia: The photos show the cave's entrance. The map was useless other than assuring us that there was a passable exit someplace. At the exit was a pool with a sign warning of crocodiles.

The Resettlement Project: We joined a group started by Gerhart Klauda to resettle beggars from the streets of Addis. Princess Meriam Senna helped us get the land shown here.

The Resettlement Project: The brave settlers headed out on a truck and after several miserable days, had this shelter.

The Resettlement Project: Our first crop.

The Resettlement Project: Street was named in my Honor.

The Resettlement Project: Bruno and Betty Lu manage expenses from the front of Bruno's office.

Move to the Big House: Blind Boys Music Club

Move to the Big House: My family moved into the house with the Philip's family.

Move to the Big House: The Street Boys loved to go out of the city for picnics.

Move to the Big House: Game behind the big house

Post Logue: There are many stories in circulation about how he died. Eventually. his body was recovered and placed here in the Holy Trinity Cathedral next to his wife.

Post Logue: We visited the Resettlement Village after about 15 years and were pleased that no children had leprosy and all were in school, one at the university.

Post Logue: The Street Boy school expanded into a network of schools, vocational training and a Hope University. We attended the first graduation.

ABOUT THE AUTHOR

I feel very fortunate to have been able to pursue two professional interests. First, I am a scientist and engineer involved in research and teaching. I participated in an international effort to build the first fusion test reactor. I was based in Japan and traveled extensively in the US, Europe and Russia.

My second interest is in living and teaching in other cultures in exotic places. The second interest developed during graduate studies when my wife and I took a three-year break to teach in Sierra Leone. We were bitten by the "wanderlust" bug, and this started a life mixed with adventure.

After graduate school, we moved to Ethiopia, a country with an ancient culture and anxious to develop their university system. I became the Department Head of Physics and was active in starting a school for street boys and a resettlement project for people recovering from leprosy.

After we left, a long period of repressive rule followed in which many of my students were imprisoned and some killed. When Ethiopia was peaceful again, I returned to continue in education, helping that humble street boy school become a university.

Printed in Great Britain
by Amazon

30548675R00086